THAI PRIVATE EYE

For more than a decade, private detective Warren Olson worked the bars and back alleys of Bangkok. Fluent in Thai and Khamen, he was able to go where other private eyes feared to tread. Although Olson has since retired from the PI scene and has returned to his native New Zealand, the company he founded in Bangkok, Thai Private Eye, is still open for business (*www.thaiprivateeye.com*).

Olson, who holds a Masters in Strategic Studies, is the co-author of *Confessions of a Bangkok Private Eye*, his first collection of case files from Thailand.

OTHER BOOKS BY WARREN OLSON

Confessions of a Bangkok Private Eye
(co-authored with Stephen Leather)

THAI PRIVATE EYE

Warren Olson

monsoon

monsoonbooks

Published in 2009
by Monsoon Books Pte Ltd
52 Telok Blangah Road
#03-05 Telok Blangah House
Singapore 098829
www.monsoonbooks.com.sg

ISBN: 978-981-08-1084-9

National Library Board Singapore Cataloguing in Publication Data

Olson, Warren, 1952-
Thai private eye / Warren Olson. – Singapore : Monsoon Books, 2009.
p. cm.
ISBN-13 : 978-981-08-1084-9 (pbk.)

1. Private investigators – Thailand. 2. Investigations. I. Title.

HV8099
363.28909593 -- dc22   OCN255892837

Printed in Singapore

12 11 10 09   1 2 3 4 5 6 7 8 9

For my daughter, Natalie

After many years, I finally left Thailand, armed with a much better understanding of life, some great memories, some lifelong friends and one jewel.

CONTENTS

PREFACE

It was in the early 1990s that, somewhat by chance, I founded what started out as a struggling private investigation agency. A decade later, in a decision most parents will understand, I decided to give up dodging bullets, bargirls, and bourbons and return to my native New Zealand, primarily for the well-being of my young daughter Natalie. During that decade, I had not only investigated many cases, but also developed a very fine understanding of Asian ways and means – in particular, Thailand's unique traditions and customs and the amazing cultural heritage of the Kingdom.

Confessions of a Bangkok Private Eye, published in 2006 by Monsoon Books, was a compilation of just some of the many cases I investigated as founder of that agency, Thai Private Eye. I was then fortunate to have renowned author Stephen Leather fictionalize (in order to protect both innocent and guilty) some of those cases and, in so doing, bring to life the people involved.

Now that I'm well settled back in New Zealand, a number of factors have inspired me to write this follow-up volume, *Thai Private Eye*. The first of these factors was the positive reception given to *Confessions of a Bangkok Private Eye*, along with the encouraging feedback I received on that book. I was certainly surprised by the range of readers the book attracted: it seems to have appealed to far more than just travellers stuck in airports or hotel rooms around Southeast Asia.

My continuing association with the current director of my old company, as both advisor and personal friend, has also kept me abreast of some more recent intriguing cases that I am now able to include here. All types of cases are chronicled here, from unfortunate tsunami-related calamities and the latest scams to wayward husbands and their vindictive wives.

These days, not only are basic investigations part of the Thai Private Eye mandate, but the agency also handles such matters as in-depth assessments for high profile multinational companies; providing security for VIPs; and the supply and placement of the very latest surveillance technology. I have to admit that the company's current operations have spread into far wider fields than I ever envisaged. Reports based on some of these more recent cases, along with a number of my older cases, all go together to make Thai Private Eye what I believe is a worthy sequel to *Confessions of a Bangkok Private Eye*.

Not being the accomplished wordsmith Stephen Leather is, I won't even attempt to enrich characters in the manner he did for me in *Confessions*. What I have tried to do, however, is to include more aspects of Asian culture, beliefs and sociology in this book.

By doing so, I hope that in addition to being an entertaining read, this book may help to reduce some of the lack of understanding that I am only too aware often exists between Westerners and Asians. By frequently adding explanations as to why certain scenarios may have unfolded as they did, I've sought, in my own small way, to narrow that cultural gap.

While writing this book, I completed a Masters degree in Strategic Studies at Victoria University (NZ) and wrote a research paper that looks at the way Western–Asian interviews and interrogations are conducted. Indeed, I now lecture on this subject. The ways people in the East and the West think and perceive things often differ greatly. This was something that became even more apparent to me when, after many years of living in Thailand and being entwined in the local culture, beliefs and language, I returned to New Zealand to be confronted by the somewhat upfront and abrupt Kiwi way of doing things. This also spurred my interest in trying to include a deeper cultural insight into the cases detailed in this book. With this volume, I hope to help our readers appreciate both Asian and Western perspectives, as very different as they may sometimes be.

Warren Olson, MSS
Wellington, New Zealand

INTRODUCTION

For a number of reasons, the writing of this book has fallen neatly into two parts.

Part One is to some extent a continuation of my earlier book, *Confessions of a Bangkok Private Eye*. The cases detailed there were ones in which I was personally involved. It is perhaps fair to say that no one will be able to emulate those early days of Thai Private Eye, and that is not just because of my own somewhat unique (or should I say eccentric?) ways.

Because of my background in the Kingdom, being the first *farang* to manage a major hotel in the poorer Northeastern or I-sarn region situated on the Thai–Cambodian border, I had little choice but to become fluent in Thai and Khamen. It also meant that I became very aware of, and often involved in, many of the local customs and beliefs.

I soon developed a great affinity with working-class Thais. I understood not just their language, but also their beliefs and dreams. I probably attended temples or visited fortune tellers as often as they did, and I found myself quite at home in small, upcountry villages eating local delicacies such as grasshoppers, common birds, or frogs, all of which were washed down with some of the very powerful homemade whiskeys that went under such wonderful names as *See sip degree* (40 degree proof); *Sip et sua* (eleven tigers); or *Sart-oh*, the sweet white liquid that, like them all, packed a very potent punch. I was therefore able to sit down in any upcountry village with a group of locals, pass myself off as a writer, travel agent, or perhaps claim I assisted in gaining visas for Thais, and get the "gossip" on a girl from that particular village. So while this procedure became almost routine for me, it was something few other foreigners could emulate.

When in Bangkok, I would venture to tourist nightspots like Hard Rock, CM Square, Spasso or other trendy hotel discos only when on a job. I was more at home at Tahwan Dang, Dance Fever or Bow Goong Pow – huge Thai nightclubs where I was not only the only foreigner, but where I was able to join in with the hearty singing of the favourite Thai pop song of the day.

One well-known song I used regularly was called "*Kitt mark*". This title refers to a common Thai term which means "think too much". Seeing a Thai girl deep in thought, I would walk by and sing the plaintive opening line, *Mai oh naa yaa Kitt mark*. This is a lighthearted, inoffensive saying that would invariably break the ice and usually get a response or a reason for the deep thinking. A foreigner simply asking "What's the problem?" would probably just get waved away.

Likewise, I had a decent collection of Thai *Soup-par-sits*, or proverbs, I could call on. Proverbs and sayings abound in everyday Thai conversation. It was not, however, only those value-added qualities that made me somewhat unique and able to often gain information more easily than it would be for my successors.

In what I loosely term the pre-Tsunami time, corruption was rife; in particular, the ease of accessing information from various agencies. Also, the Surin hotel where I had, unbeknown to me at the time, gained much of the knowledge that would be so useful to a struggling private eye had been the venue for almost all major police, army and government conferences in northeastern Thailand. When you meet almost any Thai, following the *wai* greeting you will, in most cases, be offered their name card. Fortunately, I had had the foresight to hold onto a very large number of such cards, many from influential contacts whom I was able to call on at a later date for advice or assistance.

One positive legacy of former premier Thaksin Shinawatra, who rose to prominence at that same time, was a crackdown on corruption in government departments. These reforms, much in line with international policy and anti-terrorism laws, gave wide powers to AMLO, the anti-money laundering agency, and also propelled a major revamping of the Thai police force. In this "tsunami of reforms", many former influential people found themselves moved to what people politely call an "inactive post".

These changes, along with an overall tightening of laws, including visas, banking information and transfers, and – most upsetting of all for many people – placing a closing time on bars and clubs of 2 am (when previously one could party till dawn) all resulted in things becoming rather more difficult for me and the way I was used to operating.

The big personal change, however, was the birth of my daughter Natalie in 2002.

It soon became clear to me that, as a family, we would have far better opportunities back in my native New Zealand. This was particularly clear when I considered the nature of my work and my not quite bourgeois lifestyle. We planned our departure from the Land of Smiles, and I began the slow search to find the right person to take over the daily running of Thai Private Eye. It was some time later, around the time of the tsunami disaster, that I, my wife Pathumrat, and our daughter Natalie finally left Bangkok and settled back in New Zealand.

Part Two of this book therefore looks at cases conducted after the tsunami up until the current day.

These changed times of tighter restrictions on information, less corruption, and a new guard at Thai Private Eye all mean a slightly different approach had to be used.

I remain in touch with my old firm as mentor and advisor and have not only maintained a close relationship with the new director, but also have great admiration for the way he has stepped in and coped with the daily difficulties of running an investigation company. This is especially true considering those additional problems he and his staff have faced as they had not had the same grounding I could call on.

More frequent use of state-of-the-art equipment developed especially for the investigative field is also a notable feature of the company these days, as is the appointment of a larger number of "operatives" based throughout the Kingdom.

The company has also moved into the security and personal protection fields, while the clientele itself has widened to include international companies. With all these developments, a higher profile, upmarket company has emerged. I am both honoured and proud to still be recognized as the company's founder as it enters a new level of investigations throughout Asia.

As I wanted this book to be informative as well as entertaining, I thought it important to include more recent cases as well as those from my own colourful past. I am therefore indebted to those at Thai Private Eye for their help and willingness to pass on more recent case notes to me, which we have worked on together to compile Part Two. As with all the other cases discussed in this book, they are totally based on fact, though names of places, people's names and their descriptions have been altered to protect all concerned.

PART ONE: THE EARLY YEARS

AS ONE DOOR CLOSES

*"It is usually more important how a man
meets his fate than what it is."*
Karl Wilhelm von Humboldt

I've often been asked how I ended up in the investigative business. Was I a former policeman or lawyer, perhaps an enforcement officer? Certainly not.

Born and raised in a small New Zealand town known as the "Kentucky of the Southern Hemisphere", it was not surprising that I dabbled in the thoroughbred industry for a time.

Indeed, my introduction to the Southeast Asian region, in the late 1980s, was as a would-be bloodstock agent around the racetracks of Macau, Singapore and Bangkok.

Having a grounding in hotel marketing and management as back-up, I found that field proved a more viable alternative than horses, and so, with little to keep me in the Antipodes and with the vibrant and exciting Land of Smiles beckoning, accepting a hotel management position for a Koh Samui resort was not a very difficult decision for me. Eventually, I moved on to an even better post at a hotel in Surin. By then, I had been in the Kingdom for five years and had a pretty good command of the local lingo. Everything seemed fine in my life.

What then prompted the founding of Thai Private Eye, and what were the first cases I was involved in? To answer these questions in the detail they deserve, I need to go back to the early 1990s and a hotel situated in northeastern Thailand, very close to the Cambodian border. This was not a time, nor a place, where foreign visitors were all that common.

Bear in mind that this also was a time when corruption and abuse of power were far more prevalent (and evident) in that part of Asia than they are today. Cambodia's Khmer Rouge were still a force to be reckoned with, although the brief sightings I had of them were in business deals where rights to gemstones or teak were under discussion rather than human rights and genocide.

I had unwittingly ended up in that corner of Thailand as the token white-man, managing a hotel that seemingly doubled as the meeting place for anyone in the region wanting to conduct an illicit or dodgy deal! Certainly, that is no longer the case in that locale; indeed, tourism is thriving these days, and rightly so. Temples rivalling Cambodia's famed Angkor Wat, built along the wonderful Khmer highway constructed in the 12th century, are just part of the area's unique offerings. (Amongst the other highlights flaunting the region's Khmer history and culture are the much fought-over temple of Khao Phra Viharn straddling the Thai-Cambodian border and the magnificent Wat Sikoraphum in Surin.)

I was the first Westerner, or *farang* as we are known in Thai, to be involved with a major hotel in that northeastern part of Thailand known locally as I-sarn. I was very well received and particularly well-treated by both the staff and, especially, the hotel owners. The fact I spoke Thai fluently and understood and respected the local customs obviously helped greatly in that respect. It also meant that I was privy to much more of the local ways and gossip than a casual tourist or someone just passing through would pick up on, or even suspect. I was often asked to meetings and luncheons or introduced to influential people, even included in functions or "boys' nights out" that normally were out of bounds to a *farang*.

A key attribute I have always prided myself on, being observant, was also a big factor in helping me slowly put things together and get an understanding of just what was happening around me. I also believe I have at least one other important attribute: common sense, something I tend to think is not always that common. In later years, as a private eye dealing with a wide range of clients, I became ever more convinced of how rare common sense can sometimes be! Especially during my time at that hotel, I came to learn and understand the Thai way of looking and watching, but of not saying anything detrimental to one's superiors, and certainly not doing anything to rock the boat!

That, then, briefly outlines the time, the place, and the situation I was in when I unwittingly became involved, albeit on the fringes, in what developed into a Thai national scandal. This scandal included murder, sensationalism and mayhem. It also ultimately signalled the end of my hotel career, and, in due course, the beginnings of my new career as a private eye.

Call it gossip, the "bush telegraph", or *nin tah,* as they say in Thai, but certainly news of any happening or event spreads as fast, if not faster, around backwater Thailand than in any Western country where mobile phones, i-Pods, TV and radio stations abound. Early one morning, by the time I had made my way down from my room in the hotel to my office behind the reception desk, I was bombarded with both questions and information about the arrivals who had been secreted into the hotel late the previous evening and were now ensconced in the suites up on the hallowed top floor.

Our hotel had a number of special suites that, by and large, were permanently reserved for some of the more influential local dignitaries. It was clearly understood by all the staff that what went on in the top floor suites stayed in the top floor suites, and any lack of discretion would mean loss of job. In this case, however, the news was just too big! That three blonde American movie stars were (supposedly) our latest guests had the hotel all a-buzz.

Amongst the almost three hundred staff that included the usual cast of housemaids, porters, maintenance and office workers, along with our various restaurant, nightclub and massage parlour girls, there were only three or four who spoke more than a few words of English. My interpreting skills were therefore often called upon, and so it was not too long before I was fielding calls from the supposed celebrities. It soon became evident to me that these "stars" were no doubt far more *au fait* with the Iron Curtain than with the star-spangled banner.

At that time, flights cruised between Vladivostok and the Pattaya airport of U-tapao quite regularly, as Russians, both tourists and entrepreneurs, began to flock to the seaside "city of sleaze", as it was commonly known by locals. I was fairly sure that was the route our blonde guests would have taken. I had also noted that these particular guests had not actually checked in.

Over the next few days, I would occasionally catch up with these ladies in our main restaurant. I could see why they had become, shall we say, "available to the local market". While I personally considered them presentable, they were not what I would have called glamorous; well, not at this stage of their careers anyway. They were now, I figured, well into their thirties, and at least two of them seemed to be fighting a losing battle with drugs and alcohol. The third, Vera, was the most approachable. She spoke the best English of the three, and so, over time, I gained a little knowledge of their background from her.

Her two friends were called Anna and Irina, and one way or another, the three had come under the control of the Russian mafia. Vera told me she was a qualified accountant, but had been made redundant. Her husband had left her with a young child, and she had needed to borrow money to survive.

The girls had been promised a lot of cash for a three-month trip to Thailand. It seemed like easy money in a beautiful, warm resort well away from cold, forbidding Vladivostok.

Vera left her son with his grandmother and set off in the hope of providing a better future for her family. Anna, along with her friend Irina, had lived in the same apartment building as Vera. Originally dancers, these two had been forced into more dubious methods of earning a rouble as hard times hit Russia. Arrangements were made and the girls flown to Pattaya. However, there was not so much demand for them at the resort, where the majority of tourists were from the West and preferred to play with the younger, cheaper local girls.

Their contracts had subsequently been sold to a Thai syndicate. That was how they had found themselves very far from home, in the suites of a hotel whose name they couldn't pronounce, in a region they had never heard of, and under the control of people who spoke a language they didn't understand.

I had to admit, it was an inspired business decision by those concerned, as at that time, the local economy was buoyant. We had a massage parlour at the rear of the hotel that boasted a number of worthy candidates for Miss Thailand amongst the masseuses. However, for a change, these local ladies were practically ignored by the local male population.

The closest most of the local Thai men had ever come to a blonde was at the movies or on TV. To have real live blonde women in their midst, and available for a fee, was a dream come true, and the queue to the hotel's top floor resembled the ones at McDonald's: never-ending.

Although not a feature in the more tourist-oriented or large-city hotels, a focal point at most upcountry Thai hotels is the restaurant or coffee shop, particularly at night, when diners are entertained by a string of singers. A common practice is to send, as a token of appreciation, a *mal-ai*, a type of garland, up to the singer. Guests motion to one of the ever-present young waiters or waitresses, who will quickly produce a well-worn garland of flowers. To the garland, depending on how much "face" you wish to present or how keen you are to have the singer come and join you at your table for a time, you attach some money. I have seen well-known or extremely beautiful singers be presented with garlands carrying more money than I would earn in two or three months as the hotel manager, although the normal amount would be somewhere in the US$10 - $20 range. After her song, the singer will then go to thank, and perhaps join, the *mal-ai* presenter at his or her table for a time. It is said that, at this stage, negotiations for any extracurricular activities may take place.

Our hotel boasted a very fine array of singers, some even possessing reasonable talent. One of my more enjoyable pastimes was to sit in the restaurant on quiet afternoons having a snack while the girls entertained a few late lunch guests or rehearsed for the evening. It was quite a feather in the cap of any singer if she could give an occasional rendition of a popular English song – and guess who was available as a tutor. So it was for that talent rather than my presenting any garlands that I came to have some of the more attractive singers often sitting beside me taking in my every word.

On this particular day, I had enticed the best looking of the singers to join me for an intimate language lesson; all was fine with the world, I thought. But you know what they say about the calm before the storm. We had worked through "Oceans apart day after day, and I slowly go insane, I hear your—" Then, as usual, we were struggling with the Thai pronunciation of the "v" in "voice". I had just resigned myself to settling for "woy" when "Uncle" appeared.

I'm sure "Uncle" was not telepathic, but it just took two little nods for my latest interest to grab her songbook and scuttle off while the ever-present waiter boy scurried over to deliver, in record time, a bottle of Johnny Black, two bottles of soda, two glasses, and a bucket of ice to the table.

Unlike his wealth, power and influence, Uncle's English was

limited, so we conversed in Thai. Uncle was in his mid-fifties, but still in very good shape, especially allowing for the amount of whiskey he seemed to consume. He had once told me there was not a government, armed forces unit, or police department in the entire region he did not have some influence over, and I had no reason to doubt him. Palm-greaser, fix-it man, spin doctor, Uncle was indeed a well-known, dare I say even respected, man around the place. On this occasion, however, the boot was a little bit on the other foot: Uncle apparently was having some small problems with affairs of the heart and wanted some discreet advice. This, you understand, was not in regard to any matters related to performance or such, but more into possible Western outlooks on love and marriage.

In hushed tones, the name "Irina" was mentioned, and it soon became apparent that Uncle had plans for settling back on one of his many rice plantations with a magnificent "blonde model" trophy wife as a crowning glory to his lifetime achievements.

Just what the washed-up Miss USSR thought of this wasn't clear. I quickly gathered that not only had I been selected to give him advice on how best to proceed in his quest, but also to get some feedback as to Irina's interest in this project. That the only bit Russian I had ever had the slightest interest in was the term "Smirnoff" obviously meant little to Uncle. I was of the same skin colour, so therefore I would know the key answers.

I could have mentioned the possible difficulties a high-flying, drug-addicted prostitute from one of the world's most rough-and-tumble cities might face living in a small village in northeast Thailand with a man twenty years her senior. The fact that nightclubs, beauty salons, and shopping malls were not common in that area, not to mention a surprising lack of all things Russian, sprang to mind as possible impediments. I knew, however, that it paid to placate Uncle, so I dismissed those thoughts, mentioned a few minor details about Western women and individualism, equal rights and such, then assured him I would see what I could find out regarding Irina's interest.

My now well-developed understanding of Asian ways – i.e. not saying what one really thinks or in any way rocking the boat – paid immediate dividends, as Uncle smiled, indicated the meeting was over, stood up, and passed the drink card to me. He motioned to his surly driver standing nearby, and together they left the restaurant.

I was well aware that one didn't want to be the bearer of bad news as far as Uncle was concerned, so I was not really looking forward to our next meeting. However, for the time being, I figured there was little else I could do but find Vera sometime soon and see if she had and ideas or inside information regarding Irina's interest in or opinion of the gentleman. As it transpired, I need not have worried, for I would never see Uncle again.

Not surprisingly, a call to the top floor confirmed that Miss Vera was "busy" at the moment. However, I mentioned that

Uncle had asked me to talk to her, and an hour or so later, I was told she was in the coffee shop waiting for me.

I got on well with the petite, switched-on (though maybe "calculating" was a better description) Vera. The fact that I had no designs on her whatsoever, and we both knew clearly where we stood, was perhaps the reason for this. As usual when we had a coffee together, there were a number of Thai words or phrases she had noted that she wanted explained, along with a few queries about local banks, currency, and the country in general. And then it was my turn.

I said that I had heard Irina may have had a proposal. "Oh, we get about ten a day," she blithely noted. I said that this was perhaps a serious, special proposal, and then Vera mentioned that Irina had received a gold bracelet the other day.

I pointed out that in Thailand, this could be considered *mun* or, in effect, an engagement gift that reserved the girl for the donor of the gold. I then gave her a description of Uncle, and she confirmed that, yes, he was the presenter of the gold bracelet and that he often spent the whole afternoon with Irina.

"So, do you think she would consider a life in outback Thailand?" I asked, pointing out that Uncle was very wealthy and well-connected.

"I doubt it," she laughed. "Besides, his is not the only serious proposal she has had."

That certainly sparked my interest. "So who else is chasing

the lovely Irina?" I asked.

"Moo," she said. "The young chubby guy. He hasn't given her any gold, but he does give her a lot of *yaa baa*." Vera had to get back to her waiting clients, and I had to work out just what I should tell Uncle. Was he aware that his spoilt, obnoxious, drug-dealing and fittingly named young nephew Moo was a rival for the affections of Miss Vladivostok ?

Yaa baa, Moo's regular gift to Irina, means "crazy medicine" in Thai and is a form of methamphetamine that is very popular throughout the Kingdom. It was formerly known as horse medicine, or *yaa maa*, but the media were asked to change the name so as to make it less popular, a ploy that failed. Sadly, it was originally given to many Thais, such as those engaged in the fishing, building, or sugar-cane cutting industries, by unscrupulous employers as it would allow them to work long hours without sleep. It then was adopted by the night industry, where it became better known as a recreational drug.

As to the name Moo: part of Thai tradition is that children are given a nickname that stays with them for life. The name usually relates to some food, an event, or happening when the baby is young. "Moo" means pig and is often given to chubby babies. Noi, Nit, or Lek, all meaning small, are also very common nicknames.

I had spent a day or two gathering my facts in order and debating just what to tell Uncle when yet another rumour began to circulate. This was not the whirlwind, hot-off-the-press, tell-everyone type of rumour our Russian guests had spawned, but one of those rumours whispered quietly, in discreet corners. Uncle had apparently gone missing.

Normally very reliable, he had missed one or two meetings and wasn't answering his phones. Of course, I had a possible explanation: he had simply taken Irina for a trip somewhere. I quickly sought out my friendly Russian contact Vera, just to confirm my theory. That theory was soon shot down in flames when Vera said they hadn't seen the gentleman for days; more, he had missed a planned afternoon and evening session with the intriguing Irina. As I understood it, Irina, while not totally distraught, was sad to have missed a relatively easy payday with a nice bonus.

The local police (who, of course, were well-known to all concerned) were called in, but to no avail. Uncle's driver and housekeeper had not seen him; in fact, he seemed to have vanished into thin air. After about a week, the story could no longer be contained locally, so a nationwide alert went out. A further week brought no news or sightings, so then the family, being both rich and influential, went on national TV and offered a substantial reward for any information that might lead to Uncle's whereabouts.

The phones, of course, started ringing like wild, and a flood of soothsayers and *mhor dhus* (fortune-tellers) descended on the hotel. Although the regional police chief was a regular at the hotel, he was not someone I could approach privately. However, I did get on well with one of his subordinates, so I thought it prudent to have a chat with him. He suggested I type out a report of my meeting with Uncle and any further information I had, and he would translate it into Thai and place it on file.

In retrospect, perhaps I should have kept my observations and investigations quiet, but, hey, I was (still unbeknown to myself) a private eye waiting to break out. In due course, however, my report, whilst proving helpful to police enquiries, would land me off-sides with my employers, and it was really this event that resulted in my becoming unemployed a month or two later.

One of the more astute (or should I say lucky?) amongst the fortune-tellers delving into the Disappearing Uncle saga was adamant that water featured in his disappearance. By that point, Uncle had been missing for over a month, and there had certainly been no cause to even consider paying out the very large reward on offer. Also, it had become quite apparent that any hope of finding him alive and well was now exceedingly thin. Any sort of finger-pointing at his family as a whole was not well received, however, and I gather my report had sort of placed me in that category of "finger-pointer".

The presence of the national police had meant the Russian "tourists" had quickly been moved on by their "agents", and obviously many of the dubious deals that Uncle and his family may have been party to were also either being questioned or put on hold. At the same time, a rather early summer season saw the local paddy fields dry up more quickly than usual, and it was in one of these that Uncle's body was discovered – with a bullet hole in the head. It seemed clear that Moo was implicated, which, of course, entailed a massive loss of face not just too him, but for the family as a whole. Whether or not they actually had any prior knowledge of the discovery, or were just well prepared for such an eventuality, the entire immediate family moved to avoid any further loss of face, questioning, or even any judicial process involving Moo. Almost overnight, the whole clan relocated to Europe, where they would obviously be out of reach. All related businesses, the hotel included, were sold.

The hotel manager was informed his services were no longer required. (Redundancy pay, you should understand, certainly did not feature in the Thai vocabulary in those days. For that matter, such courtesies are not known in Thailand even now.) As far as I know, Uncle's case was then closed, in the way such unpleasant matters could be "closed" back then.

So there I was, a hapless *farang* without gainful employment. But I am a great believer that all things happen for a reason, and my firing was actually a great stroke of luck. Before the axe fell, I had done some "checking" on one or two Thai girls for acquaintances and some related minor jobs for a few local embassies. More, whenever a tourist overheard me speaking Thai,

I was usually bombarded with questions. I started to think that it was worth considering if I could perhaps put my local knowledge to use in a way that might help to pay the rent.

It was not long after that, while sitting at a small table on the corner of Sukhumvit Road Soi 13 in Bangkok, along with a good friend and an ample supply of Thai whiskey, that the idea of Thai Private Eye came to me. Shortly thereafter, the idea came to fruition.

COPS AND ROBBERS

"Corruption is nature's way of restoring our faith in democracy."
Peter Ustinov

It was not the classic orange sunrise one sees in the Northeast, but a dull glow as the sun forced its way through the Bangkok smog. Almost on cue, an amber-robed monk came round the corner of the *soi*, bearing his alms bowl. Not having the usual Thai gift of food to give him, I instinctively dug into my pocket for a 100-baht note and placed it in the bowl with a respectful *wai*. Surely some good karma would come to me today; maybe that cute new waitress at my local Starbucks might succumb to my charms? One last picture on the mobile, forward it, and I was off for a decent sleep.

It's very rare that I do work prior to payment, but in this case, Rob was a reliable and trustworthy customer – which is much more than could be said about his current Thai girlfriend. Rob had called from the UK that evening, just after speaking to the lovely Miss Pookie, who had told him she was off to a friend's birthday party, but sure she'd be back in her apartment by 2 am. Rob assured me a retainer would be on its way first thing in the morning, but could I check the apartment from 1 am to 6 am, just to confirm Pookie's presence. Having done surveillance on Pookie in the past, I knew she was too young, too pretty, and far too keen on a good time to be sitting home alone like the Macaulay Culkin character, waiting for Rob's return. I wish I was as sure about next week's lotto numbers as I was of a "no-show" by Pookie at her apartment.

I sent Rob off a final picture of the apartment window, adding that there had still been no sign of his beloved, and motioned over to one of the nearby taxi-motorcycle boys, who must have been wondering what the hell this crazy *farang* (Westerner) was doing sitting on a concrete slab outside a low-class Thai apartment block all night. At least daybreak is one time of day when Bangkok's roads are relatively quiet, and 15 minutes later I was back at my apartment in the small street, or *soi*, of Rangnam.

A quick shower to wash away some Bangkok grime, and then crash into bed. If you believe private eyes enjoy a glamorous lifestyle, you have obviously spent more time reading books or watching movies than you have being employed as one!

About the same time, TG 994 from Sydney was touching down at Bangkok's Don Muang Airport. Dave couldn't wait to get off the plane and back to places he had been dreaming about for the past six months. This would be his third trip to the Land of Smiles; he was almost an old hand now, he reckoned. He knew some basic Thai, he knew you didn't ever pay the asking price for anything, and he also knew the lay of the land around the bar- and girl-packed Sukhumvit Road. His usual guide/mentor was not with him this trip, but that made it all the more exciting: three weeks at the Ambassador Hotel, free to come and go when he wanted, with whatever bargirl took his fancy! Being in one's mid-forties, but able to act like mid-twenties is what Bangkok is all about to the majority of Caucasian male tourists!

In another part of town, Noi woke up as the bus pulled into the Bangkok bus terminal, or Mor Chit, along with dozens of other buses from Thailand's Northeast. This callow teenager had just taken the overnight trip to Bangkok from I-sarn. I-sarn is the Thai name for the vast, mostly poor, northeastern region of Thailand that supplies most of the "working girls" in Bangkok bars. It also supplies the majority of the city's taxi drivers as well as factory and construction workers.

Noi was a slight girl with a cute face somewhat darkened by the I-sarn sun, a little taller and perhaps more developed than many Thai 15-year-olds, which seems to be a common trait for those with a Thai-Cambodian heritage. She had on a loose-fitting black T-shirt and her favourite pair of blue jeans. (Genuine Levis, her sister had told her when she gave them to her on her last visit home.)

Noi's older sister was now living in Switzerland, so the regular gifts to the family had slowed a little of late. Pee Sai ("older sister", though this particular lady was actually an auntie) had spoken to Noi's mum and said that she would take care of the young girl and see she kept up the family tradition of being a dutiful daughter and sending regular payments back to Buriram.

Noi took her small backpack down from the overhead locker, and made her way off the bus, a sparkle in her eyes. She had hopes of an adventure about to begin, with the tales told to her by her sister and Pee Sai of rich, handsome foreigners packing huge amounts of cash foremost in her mind. She, too, glanced at the hazy sunrise as she walked towards the waiting taxis: nothing as spectacular as the sunrises she had seen over the famed Khao Phanom Rung temple back in her home province, but that was all behind her now. She was about to become free and rich.

It didn't take Noi long to adapt to the Soi Nana bar scene. Pee Sai was, in fact, the *mamasan* at a small bar up on the second level. (The Thai *mamasan*, herself often a former working girl, is in charge of all the girls in a bar. She gets commissions on their earnings, and if she has a number of girls at her call, can be in strong demand from other bar owners.) An elderly German was the owner, but he was not often around, and usually drunk when he was. The girls who worked there thus had a fairly easy life and were for the most part themselves drunk or drugged on *yaa baa*.

Noi had indeed experienced drink, drugs, and sex back in her village, a reason her parents were not sad to send her off to Bangkok. But her experiences back home were nothing on the scale of the activities she was to witness in the Nana Plaza, which is probably more popular than the Patpong area these days, as a bar, go-go dancer and night-time entertainment centre.

Officially a "glass washer" – girls are supposed to be 18 before being allowed to work as dancers – Noi had after a few days already begun earning "extra" as a number of Japanese clients had been allowed to venture to the small upstairs room with her, under Pee Sai's guidance, all assured that young Noi was indeed virginal, and that a short-time fee of 5,000 baht was a real bargain.

To maintain the long hours of dance, drink and sex, *yaa baa* was all but mandatory amongst the girls. Noi had seen it used back in the village by labourers or those working long hours in the rice fields during harvest, so it was no big deal to sneak to the upstairs room with some of the others, see the small chocolate-smelling orange tab produced and placed in some tin foil, with a lighter deftly positioned underneath, and then take her turn at inhaling the resulting smoke.

Although Noi had been working for just over a week, she fitted into the routine like she was born to it – and, in fact, she probably was. On the particular day events surrounding this case actually began, perhaps the German owner had been drinking too much

45

and forgotten his weekly "payment" to the local constabulary, or maybe the establishment next door was simply jealous of the bar's upsurge in business.

The girls themselves decided later that it was because they had forgotten to pay respects to Buddha that day, although at the time they didn't think so, as there was a group of Japanese guys in the bar spending money like it was water. However, the usual lookout was not on duty, so Noi had no time to dart off to hide in the upstairs room when, late in the afternoon, in strode two plainclothes Thai policemen. The Japanese were quickly ushered outside, all the girls ID's were taken, they were marched out and herded into the back of a pick-up, and a heavy chain was locked around the bar doors.

Most of the girls were able to pay a "release fee" at the local station once they had completed a drug test and had all their details recorded. Those testing positive for drugs would have a much higher fee to pay. If they didn't have the money, or were repeat offenders, it would mean at least a 100-day prison sentence.

As the last few paragraphs suggest, baksheesh or bribe money was a Thai way of life back then. Note that this case relates to circa 2000, and attempts have been made to clean up the image and the Thai police departments since then. But not too long ago, police precincts were to an extent self-supporting and relied on various forms of payments or "taxes" from most businesses within their region.

Noi's life suddenly took the worst turn ever: she was singled out by two of the officers, and they were not looking at her kindly. The facts were spelt out clearly: she was working in a bar, under-age, and also under the influence of drugs. She was certainly old enough to be sentenced in Thailand, and, in fact, she would probably be looking at 200 days in total. Noi was totally distraught; not only was the shame of a jail spell hanging over her head, but that would also mean she could not send money back to her family during that time. There was, said a large policeman, one possible way out of this; what's more, if she cooperated, they would even supply Noi with a mobile phone!

Dave, meanwhile, was having the time of his life. He had a regular routine, and this day, as usual, he had got up just in time to catch the complimentary breakfast, read the papers, do a little shopping, and by mid-afternoon, he was ready to start a new adventure, so he made his way to Soi 7 and the Beer Garden, a well known hangout for P4Ps, as they are called. That "P4P" stands for "pay for play girls": in effect, short-time freelance prostitutes.

Some were bargirls on their way to work who wanted some extra cash for their drug habit, others did not want the restrictions of having to go to work daily, whilst some did have a poorly paid job at a factory or food stall, but often needed additional earnings. All sorts were to be found in the vicinity of Sukhumvit Road, Soi 7.

As Dave sat at the bar and ordered the first Heineken of the day, a fairly tired selection of Thai girls eyed him – they had seen him in there the last few days and by now knew he was not an easy target. Dave recognized an Aussie accent beside him and struck up a conversation with Ray, who he learnt was himself from Sydney. A regular to Thailand, he brought clothing from Bo-Bey market, he told Dave, and then sold it at the weekend markets back home. They chatted away, each happy to have some engaging company; one thing about Thai girls, it's not easy to find one you can discuss rugby or the Melbourne Cup with, or come to think of it, anything much other than money, food, and … ummm, money!

During a toilet break, Dave had noticed a small sticker strategically placed above the Beer Garden urinal. "Thai Private Eye" it read. He mentioned the sticker to Ray, who said yes, he had heard about the guy, and he apparently did a good job. They joked about the possibilities and the fact that it was one service savvy guys like themselves would certainly not require.

Ray had to go, so they swapped mobile numbers, and agreed to meet up the next afternoon. Dave finished off his Heineken and was debating his next move when he saw the cutest little Thai girl hovering by the entrance. She glanced at him, flashed the flicker of a smile, then lowered her eyes. Dave thought he had already had enough experience to know this was not a seasoned working girl, and he soon sauntered over and introduced himself.

Young and fresh, with a cheeky grin, she told Dave that she was waiting for her friend – and when he suggested they go wait in his hotel room, she said okay and took his hand as he led her back to the Ambassador Hotel. Being early afternoon, the leeching night manager who was usually able to draw an "extra" 500 baht out of most male tourists bringing "unchecked-in guests" back to their rooms late at night was nowhere to be seen. In a matter of minutes, Ray and the young lady had made their way up to his room.

Noi (yes, it was our former innocent from I-sarn) had quickly announced she "take shower". She may be young, thought Dave, but true to type; she obviously knows what's in store! She came out five minutes later, wrapped up in a hotel towel, told Dave it was his turn now, took the TV remote, found a Thai channel, and climbed into bed. Dave didn't waste much time in the shower. He was soon out, wrapped in a towel, and climbing in beside her. And then …

There was not even a knock: suddenly the door burst open, and two plainclothes policemen were in the room, barking out orders. "You – *farang* – get clothes quick!" Dave was completely shell-shocked. He hardly noticed Noi scuttling off to the bathroom and just as quickly disappearing out the hotel room door.

Dave quickly went on the attack: "I'll call the manager, you have the wrong room, what are you doing bursting in like that—"

The bigger and uglier of the two cops held up a hand to

silence him. He pulled a Thai ID card from his back pocket, and waved it in Dave's face. The garlic breath was overpowering, but nothing compared to the news Dave received next! "This girl's ID card say this girl 15 year old. Law in Thailand, lady must 18, go to hotel room. You come with us now."

The anticipation of an exciting afternoon had immediately vanished. Dave's head was spinning as he tried to understand what had happened, and how. More importantly, what was going to happen next? The two Thais stood close by as Dave awkwardly pulled on jeans and a T-shirt, pocketed his wallet, passport and his mobile phone and, before long, found himself at a nearby police station. He was ushered him into a tiny room that had a small, school-type desk and two chairs, and told to sit. Garlic Breath, who had slightly the better English of the pair, told him, "Fifteen year girl in room, you – you go jail long time." Then, pulling some papers out of the desk, he laboriously copied down details from Dave's passport. "You – wait here," Dave was told, then the pair walked out, a heavy metal door was pushed shut, and he heard that frightening sound of a bolt being flung into place.

With visions of a sentence at the notorious "Bangkok Hilton" prison swimming in his head, Dave wondered just who to call for help. He didn't have the embassy number; the embassy would have been shut in any case, so …

He flicked through the names on his contact list, but as he was using a Thai SIM phone card, they were mostly of bargirls, who would hardly understand him, let alone be of help. Ay, Boo, Dah, Goong, Lek, Mem ... a new number, with R beside it. Ray, the fellow Aussie he had met at the Beer Garden. Dave called him. Ray answered immediately; he was with his regular Thai girlfriend, at the real Hilton! Just the mention of the name "Hilton" sent a shudder down Dave's spine. He didn't go into the full details with Ray, just said he was in a spot of bother with the local police, what did he suggest. Ray told him the first thing was to get someone onside who spoke Thai. But Dave knew nobody in that category – apart from the bargirls. So Ray said, what about that Thai private eye, maybe he can help.

The end result was that Ray went down to the hotel computer, looked up the website, found a mobile number, text messaged Dave back, and that was how I ended up receiving a somewhat desperate phone call, just as I was getting settled into a bottle of Jack Daniels at Gulliver's Pub and about to enjoy watching Manchester United play some minnows in the FA Cup.

(Of course, being a born and bred Kiwi, I shouldn't even mention my interest in the "round-ball" game. But as rugby rarely features on Thai TV, and every Bangkok taxi driver knows all the Premiership teams off by heart, one sort of gets caught up in the trend. On top of that, I was getting special attention from a cute new waitress.)

Dave was certainly stressing out. However, I had heard some whispers about the situation he was in, and I also knew Thai procedure: regardless of who he called, or what he did, Dave was going to spend at least one night in the local holding cells. This was a sort of standard "softening-up" procedure, and even if you do call your embassy, under Thai law, you can be held for three days without even being charged. Of course, I didn't pass that information onto Dave just then. Besides, the game had just kicked off, and I already had the new waitress' mobile number!

Dave happened to mention my three favourite words – "money no object" – so I told him, "Okay, I will take the case," and promised to call by the station as soon as I could.

By the time I had seen off Man U, the bottle of JD, and the waitress, it was about 3 am, but Bangkok never sleeps, and I did feel the need to replenish some of the burnt-off calories.

I walked up Soi Rangnam, found my trusty late-night footpath food seller, and had a quick *Kow Pad Goong* (fried rice and prawns), which set me back about a single US dollar, and then found a motorcycle taxi to run me down to the police station. I got the driver to stop at a 7-Eleven and grabbed a six-pack of Coke, a stack of sandwiches and some packs of gum. I knew three things for sure: that Dave would still be at the jail, that he would have had his mobile phone taken away, and that he would be hungry and not asleep!

The duty officer had his feet up on the desk, and was watching a Thai movie on a small TV. I asked him if it featured Nong Natt (a well-known Thai porn star), then said, "*Kooey gun gup farang khap*," telling him I wanted to talk to the Westerner. I handed over 200 baht, just to save myself from any speeches about visiting hours or the perfunctory "Come back in the morning" reply.

He dragged his feet off the desk, had a quick look through the plastic 7-Eleven bag I showed him, took out a can of Coke for himself, then motioned for me to follow and led me down a narrow hallway, towards the back of the building. Solid steel bars formed a wall, beyond which there were three cells set out in an L-shape, and a small area that served as washroom: i.e., a hole in the floor with a small plastic bucket hanging over a tap. All three cell doors were open, so you could wander between them. That was just as well, as there were at least a dozen people there in total, and the cells were about 12-foot square, with no windows, bedding or furniture – just concrete and bars. There was a double row of bars along the front, so I could only get within four or five feet at best of my client. A guard was dozing in an adjacent room, but quickly showed signs of life when his duty officer and I approached.

Mutterings of *"Farang, farang"* filtered through the cellblock as I approached. The stark white – well, grimy white – skin of Dave showed out clearly amongst the drunks and drug addicts he had been thrown in with.

Dave was up against the bars in a flash. "TPE," I said, introducing myself; it seems I was better known by my company initials than my own name around most of Thailand.

"Where can we talk?" he asked.

"This is it," I told him as I passed the plastic bag across to the guard, who in turn looked in, took a Coke for himself, then went over and slid a small slide back before passing the remaining cans, sandwiches and gum through to Dave.

"Thanks," he muttered as he ripped open a Coke. "Only had a bottle of warm water and some foul-tasting rice since I've been here."

"After a few days, the rice tastes better," I told him. Not the most comforting words in that situation, I realise. But how did I happen to know about the improvement in taste? Don't ask!

Most of the Thai inmates were sleeping, though one had staggered up to see what was going on. Nonetheless, I told Dave to go ahead with his story, which was how I came to learn his side of what I have detailed.

Dave, of course, wanted instant release and the embassy on the case – as well as any other agency I could suggest. However, I explained that this would not happen, as it was, after all, now 4 am, and he was to all intents guilty. I promised I would make what inquiries I could, but as I told him, any hope of an early release would probably depend on his ability to raise funds, and fast!

This was also an opportune time to remind him of my daily fee. I explained that he had to face at least another ten or twelve hours inside, and that I would have to speak to the arresting officers before I could do much at all. They were both on day shift and would be back around 10 am. I jotted down what particulars I could. I had a full name, address, contacts in Australia, and also details of his hotel and some scant details and a description of Miss Noi: young, cute, long black hair. Of course; that description fits about half the girls in Bangkok. In short, I didn't see much hope down that avenue. But being the thorough private eye that I am, I took down all the information available.

By then, the night's activities were starting to hit me as well, so I told Dave to get what sleep he could, and I would see him around midday. He had assured me that his Visa card was in reasonable shape, so although I couldn't guarantee anything, when he asked if he would be out at midday, I just promised to do my best, and left a somewhat sombre Dave to ponder over the joys of holidaying in the Land of Smiles, especially when one allows the lower parts of one's anatomy to rule over the higher parts!

The alarm woke me just after 10 am, and I remembered Dave. It was almost midday when I returned to the station with two bottles of Johnny Walker (Black Label, of course!) in a carry-all bag and asked to see either of the officers who had brought Dave in.

In order to live, or at least live relatively hassle-free, in any Asian country, one has to understand the local ways and means. In most cases, it's all about face: negotiation is always possible, but you must always leave your opposite number some room to manoeuvre. At that moment, I figured Dave had some room, although he probably didn't know it. To call for the embassy, or the newspapers, and scream "set-up", "corruption" or "entrapment" may get you a hearing in the West, but not here. No, the only viable approach was to have a friendly chat with the two nice, hard-working, genuinely committed police officers who had brought Dave in, and to figure out a compromise. I gathered it was Garlic Breath who appeared a few minutes later and ushered me into a small office. I gave my most polite *wai* and thanked him in Thai for seeing me, then slid the carry-all bag over the desk.

Garlic Breath looked at me expectantly. Fortunately, I had a fair idea of how to proceed.

"There is a rather stupid *farang* you are holding," I said, speaking Thai so there was no chance of any misunderstanding. "This man has asked me to serve as interpreter for him. I have told him that he has done something very wrong by the Thai people, and Thai law, and he is very sorry for this mistake he made. He would like to ask you to perhaps give him a chance, and he also wishes to offer some restitution for the loss of time and the problems he has caused you."

Garlic Breath picked his nose for a moment, then held up five fingers. "*Muen?*" (Thai word for tens of thousands) I asked. He nodded. I thanked Garlic Breath again, and asked if I could have a brief chat with Dave.

Our compromise had been arranged: Garlic Breath had barely spoken a word, and I had made sure he hadn't needed to directly indicate any form of bribery. Now it was up to Dave. I had no doubts he would accept the offer, and if he did not have the money, or wanted to protest further, I was also sure he would find little joy in fighting the Thai judicial system, especially as all legal proceedings would be held in the Thai language, and he certainly would face 200 to 400 days in jail.

Dave was hunched up in a corner, trying as best one can to sleep in a concrete cell with lights on and another half dozen inmates plus a few hundred cockroaches in close proximity. He soon jumped up when I called his name and was over to the bars in a flash.

"You have to get me out of here," he pleaded. Already his eyes were sunken, he hadn't washed or shaved, and he frankly smelled worse than Garlic Breath. I wondered if he had even bothered to use the hole in the floor!

I explained the situation to him, that for a 50,000 baht "fine", the officer would be prepared to overlook his indiscretion. Otherwise, he would be charged and have to face the consequences. Dave was nodding his head, agreeing so fast, I could have told him the fine was 100,000 baht. However, I said I would need his bankcard and PIN, and would need to draw out 60,000 baht – which included 10,000 to cover my fee – and that hopefully I could do that all in one day. Dave gave me the card and details.

Yes, I did notice a flicker of doubt cross his face, but in the end, he had no choice. Guess he was lucky he had found a private eye like myself who had.. well, basically, good morals.

I tapped on Garlic Breath's door on the way out. He was studying the *Thai Rath*, a popular daily newspaper that deals in sensationalism. I told him I would be back in an hour, and perhaps he could look at Dave's paperwork in the meantime.

What with the hassles at the bank, and the Bangkok traffic, it was late afternoon before I finally returned. Garlic Breath was out, I was told, and he would only be back at 7 pm. "By which time the Station Captain would have gone home," was my cynical thought. Anyway, little to do but return later. At least there are always plenty of ways to fill in an hour or two in Bangkok, especially when I had an extra 10,000 baht in hand!

A few hours later, Garlic Breath and I were discussing the merits of Liverpool and Man U over a Johnny Walker and soda, Dave's 50,000 baht making a slight bulge in the top pocket of the officer's jacket, when Dave was brought in. Any movement, even around the station, requires prisoners to be manacled. Dave would have the cuffs on until his release was completed. I had seen similar transitions a few times: from disbelief at the time of arrest, to anger, to resentment, and then to the hope this was a bad dream that would soon be over.

Garlic Breath then began his speech, in the best English he could muster. "My fren you," he said, pointing at me with his glass, "tell me you no unnerstan Thai law, an lady Thai tell you she 18. This is statement of case, it in Thai, but say you found in your hotel room, with a girl age18. I make that alteration for you, because your fren ask me to. You sign this document, and also another document that say you have been well treated here and have not been asked to make any payments. If you do not sign, or if you go and talk to the newspapers or people about your case, I will then cross out "18" and put back "15", then we come find you. Unnerstan?" Dave understood.

The manacles were unlocked, Dave signed on the dotted line, turned down Garlic Breath's offer of a drink, and obviously wanted to get as far away as he could, as quickly as he could.

I gave a final *wai* and thanked the officer for his help. So yes, maybe there had been a significant donation to his, or, I suspect, the precinct's retirement fund, but as we say in Thailand, "TIT; this is Thailand". In recent years, much of the corruption has been eliminated, but nonetheless, if you put yourself in a suspect position, be prepared for the consequences, and don't expect to be treated as you may be in your own country.

Having noted Noi's family name off the papers at the station, in the following weeks, I kept an eye out for her when I was in the vicinity of the Beer Garden. Although Bangkok has a moving population of around 10 million, it is surprising how small it can be, and it wasn't too long before I found Miss Duangjai Booarean, aged 15, born in Buriram Province, sauntering down

Soi 7, Sukhumvit road, early one afternoon.

Okay, so I had called out "Duangjai ?" to three or four young Thai girls in the area previously, only to be met with blank looks, but this time, there was no doubt: I had found the wayward Miss Noi. The look in her eyes told me she hadn't given up using *yaa baa*, but she was certainly alert enough to wonder how I knew her name.

I took her over to a nearby seafood outlet, ordered my favourite spicy snack of *goong shar nam pla* (a popular Thai snack of raw prawns marinated in a mix of lemon juice and chilli), two cans of Coke, and then heard Noi's story.

Just to get her started, I told her that Dave had posted her picture and story on the Internet, and that he had also suggested that someone take her to a hotel and beat her up. Alright, that wasn't true, but I wanted to frighten off young Noi – for her own benefit as much as for any more naive tourists that might fall for the same trap.

So that was how I got her background and found out how she came to set up Dave and, she admitted, about a dozen others. I thought perhaps I should check to see if any had failed to pay the "fine", but I figured if that was the case, it was too late now. I asked Noi if she had any money. She opened her wallet and showed off three 1000 baht notes, which was more than I had in mine! I told her to go get the evening bus back to Buriram, and not to return to the city until she was 18, as there may well be some evil *farangs* out there looking for her.

As far as I know, she did go back to her village, although no doubt it would have only been for a while. She had had a taste of the big-city nightlife, the camaraderie, the easy money. The fact that she and, directly because of her, a number of tourists had narrowly escaped a harrowing experience in a Thai jail would soon be forgotten, especially as the back-breaking rice-planting season loomed back in the village.

CHILD'S PLAY

"A man never stands as tall as when he kneels to help a child."
Knights of Pythagoras

Let me just give you a little insight into the trials and tribulations of being a private eye when, by and large, you are operating on behalf of clients who live thousands of miles away and are used to an entirely different set of rules, regulations and cultural behaviour.

There are many times when the clients – they who are always right, even when they are wrong – don't understand the background to a situation, or cannot fathom why certain people may be acting in a certain way. When you live, as I did, for a long period of time in Thailand and become as much Asian as Western; when you instinctively take off your shoes upon entering a home; when you look with disdain at anyone raising his or her voice in public; accept that bribery and corruption are a way of life; and you know that less than 4% of the population pay taxes while unemployment or old-age benefits are totally out of the question, you do develop a deeper understanding of certain patterns of behaviour. In this respect, one tends to become not just a cultural advisor, but also a guide, a mentor; even, at times, a psychiatrist, it seems.

I had set the alarm for 5 am, time to shower, go have a quick breakfast at the 24-hour Foodland on Sukhumvit Road Soi 5, and get out to the airport to catch the early flight to Ho Chi Minh, with an onward to Nha Trang. I walked out of Foodland and up to the corner to get a taxi, and there, hanging about with two or three other down-and-out desperates trying to squeeze some easy income out of a wayward tourist, was Lee.

I reckon I had first seen the lovely Miss Lee about 10 years back, in the days when I was a marketing manager for some of the Kingdom's resort hotels, and she certainly was a young lovely back then. She had a string of regular sponsors in those days and certainly was much in demand. (For the uninitiated, a sponsor is a man who provides monthly payments to a Thai girlfriend, presumably to keep her studying or otherwise away from bar work.)

Lee was a true country girl, loved her family, and although she had numerous offers, had no intention of marrying someone and living overseas. She thought, however, that one of her beaus would be happy to live in a small village up near the Laos border with her, where they would raise a family and live happily ever after.

Well, it seemed the first few stages of Lee's dream were realised: she had had a number of affairs over the years, with the result that now, at the age of 30, she had four children, all from different fathers, three of them Westerners. Unfortunately for her and the children, the guys involved were all long gone. Perhaps some made an occasional money transfer to her bank, but certainly not very often. Consequently, every few months, when they had no money for food, Lee would leave the children with her mother in their small shack in Nong Khai province and take the twelve-hour bus trip to Bangkok, where she would basically sleep on the street, or do whatever she could to find a few customers and earn some money to take back home.

To see a formerly stunning young girl who was once the life and soul of some of the city's top night spots reduced to almost begging on street corners was a stark reminder of how tough life can be in Thailand, and how fortunes can change. I slipped her a few hundred baht for olds times' sake, then flagged down a nearby taxi.

It was just after mid-day when we touched down at Nha Trang airport; a few older outbuildings and a very long runway were clear reminders of who had built the airport. I almost expected a few Vietcong to be sniping at us from up in the hillsides as we disembarked.

I ignored the three-wheeled bicycle taxi (*samlors*) lined up outside Arrivals, as I needed to stretch my legs and it was only a five-minute walk around the corner to the Dream Hotel. The Dream may not be quite 5-star reverie, but at US$12 a night, it sounded fine to me, and so it proved.

The first sight of the beautiful Nha Trang beach was quite amazing. I guess I had become too used to the grime of Bangkok, but this Vietnamese location certainly was a lovely seaside resort, fronted by a large theme park, pools and palm trees. I had been hired by a New Zealand insurance company which had a claim from a Vietnamese lady living there against a large amount of gold jewellery bought in Nha Trang that had been stolen. She had provided the insurance company with receipts; my brief was to confirm their authenticity.

I had been put in touch with "Jack", who just happened to own Jack's Bar. I soon discovered that Jack's had a most agreeable happy hour at its rooftop beer garden every evening. Sitting back there looking out over the lush hillsides and sparkling sea, one could hardly believe this had been a war zone just a few decades previously. Jack had also found me an excellent guide. "Mary" was 39, very pleasant, spoke excellent English, and was waiting for her German boyfriend to complete her visa formalities so she could retire to the Rhine. I truly hoped he didn't let her down, as she was a nice lady.

It took a couple of days to get around to all the gold shops I needed to check out in the main part of the town, which was a few miles from the seaside, but it was a straightforward investigation and all the shops I visited were able to confirm that the receipts were indeed valid.

Of course, with the day's work done, it was only natural that I carried out a little night-time investigating of my own accord, and I was reliably informed that the Sailing Club was the place to go.

I spurned the offers of numerous motorcycle riders who came alongside me on fake Hondas offering me amazing deals for US$5 as I wandered down to the Sailing Club. But once inside the Club, I was thinking perhaps I shouldn't have been so hasty with my refusals. The place was almost deserted. If this was the best of Nha Trang nightlife, it was going to be an early evening. The bar manager told me in reasonable English that the weekends were the best time to come, and that girls from the local university often came in. This perked up my interest, until he added that it was currently a term break and most students would have gone back to their homes upcountry.

There was an American couple at the bar, so I ended up having a drink with them. I soon found out that Betty and Rory were from San Diego and were not your average backpacker Vietnam tourists or returning Vietnam vets. In their late thirties, they appeared affluent and rather quiet, compared to many Americans I seemed to meet. Rory was in the IT field, and although I didn't usually offer my profession readily, this time there seemed to be no harm in it. I passed over a card which, I noted, sent Betty's eyebrows up an inch or two when she read it.

Call it professional instinct, but I always seem to know when a job is in the air. I sensed my new friends might need a little discussion time, so I ordered another round and said I needed a toilet break. Sure enough, when I returned a few moments later, our drinks had been served on a patio table overlooking the water, well away from everyone else. There were a few background questions and the word "discretion" was thrown into the conversation more than once. I assured them I was the soul of that virtue, and added that I was pretty much able to offer suggestions on how anything in the region could be handled.

That obviously put them at ease, and so a few minutes later, I got the "We have friends who could need help in a rather delicate matter" gambit – which, of course, meant Betty and Rory themselves. But having already noted Rory's Gold Amex card, I was happy to sit back and nod my head knowingly.

The "friends" were a kind, successful couple who were only missing a baby in their lives, and they had been advised that the woman would be unable to conceive naturally. They had considered various options, and although adoption was a possible solution, that was not always easy. Besides, what they were keen on was possibly finding a surrogate mother. That way, at least one of them would be involved as biological parent. And they had heard that perhaps in Vietnam a willing party could be contacted?

I had to think this over, as one can't rush these things. (Okay, my think lasted about 20 seconds.) I then told them that perhaps they should consider Thailand ... Oops, I forgot to say "their friend" should consider it, but it went by unnoticed, as they eagerly asked for more information.

The main reason, I said, is that Thailand does not have any law against either parent taking a child out of the country. This is a law that I obviously needed to know, as when one is a private eye based in Bangkok, one does get asked to assist in all sorts of projects. And I mean *all* sorts – as you will see a little later!

Actually, I said, I do perhaps have the ideal person. "What sort of fee were you thinking of?"

"We thought US$10,000" said Rory, "plus, of course, all the expenses incurred – lawyers, doctors, hospitals."

Close to half a million Thai baht, I thought, a 10% set-up fee for Mr TPE, and that could leave ... mmmmm, let me think... And like a cartoon character with a light bulb beaming over his head, "Lee", with enough to build a family home and educate her children, flashed for me. I don't normally like playing God – but it did seem like an opportunity to help a few people in very different parts of the world realize their dreams.

I got details from Rory and Betty, and arranged to meet them in Bangkok a few days later, along with Lee and a Thai lawyer. It was agreed that a US$500 upfront fee for locating Lee and setting up the meeting would be paid into my account the next day. (I hoped Lee would still be in Bangkok.) I was becoming rather fond of Nha Trang, although disappointed that none of the local university students were on hand to avail themselves of my charms!

Thai girls tend to be pretty much creatures of habit, and sure enough, two nights later I located Lee near her usual corner. "Come into my office," I said, and escorted her to the nearby Starbucks. There, I clearly outlined what was on my, Rory's, and Betty's minds.

The mention of half a million baht sent Lee into raptures. That was the sort of windfall you only got by winning the lottery in Thailand. In fact, I'm sure she would have been happy with an offer of far less, but I figured she was due for a change of luck, as, like most of the girls working in Bangkok, she was actually a good person at heart.

As far as I am aware, all went according to plan in this instance. I did not get too involved other than appearing at the official meeting and making arrangements for Rory and Betty to rent an apartment in Nong Khai. They had my number and details and promised to keep me posted on how things went. I tend to believe it was just one of those right time-and-place coincidences that seem to abound in Asia, and I was quite happy to wish them all well and move on.

My Thai lawyer/fix-it man of course had "friends" who were doctors, interpreters, immigration specialists, nannies, etc, so I'm sure he and his family all made out well out from Rory and Betty, who, I trust, also got what they were after. I never saw Lee back on a Bangkok street corner looking destitute again, so I hope she invested wisely and her family is a little more secure these days.

Thais have a phrase which I thought relevant in this situation: *wen gum*, which basically is the Buddhist equivalent of "Do unto others as you would have them do unto you" coupled with "What goes around comes around." I knew that Lee would not under normal circumstances be able to provide any of her children the type of education and lifestyle Rory and Betty could, and if I had been one of her offspring, I would have jumped at the chance of a life in the West.

I did get a few further requests to find surrogate mothers following that encounter; perhaps from word of mouth? It is something that does happen in Asia with a little more regularity than officials possibly let on. But although this episode went smoothly, it was not something I was really comfortable with, so I passed on all further offers.

Perhaps it had something to do with that particular month, but soon after this, I also had correspondence with an obviously furtive, older Swiss gentleman who I knew was, as is often the case, only telling me half the story. He questioned me on possible methods of getting back his purported son, who was living with his Thai mother's family in Chantaburi. As far as I was concerned, It amounted to a basic kidnapping, so although he mentioned very large amounts of euros that could have seen TPE frequenting the more upmarket "Coyote" bars that were springing up all over the city rather than my usual lower-class haunts, that was a step too far – even for me!

Suffice it to say that what details I had, I passed on to my friends at Soi Suan Phlu, the address of the Thai Immigration Office. Besides, I seem to have more of an affinity with struggling factory workers and bargirls than the overpaid, over made-up, unappreciative, Hi-So (short for "high society") play-for-pay girls that were the star attraction at those trendy new Coyote bars with exorbitant prices seemingly aimed mainly at wealthy Asian tourists.

In addition to being overpriced, those girls at the Coyote Bars (modelled on the Coyote Ugly movie) very seldom leave with customers, they cannot be bar-fined, though they will give out a phone number and sometimes meet guys outside of working hours – where fees of about ten times the norm are the usual starting point!

Most cases involving children tend to be difficult, and I did find myself being asked to participate in such cases more than a few times. Unfortunately, there are those Thai families who basically hold the *Luk-Krung* (the Thai name given to a child of mixed Thai/Western parentage) to ransom, knowing the child can be the source of a steady cash flow. However, by and large, Thais maintain very close and loving families and typically offer a more stable environment than would the wayward "alleged" father! Indeed, in Thailand, children of a mixed Thai/Western heritage are somewhat revered, and many of the Kingdom's entertainers, singers, movie stars are all from that type of mixed background.

But case of Harry, another client with child troubles, provides a good example of what can go wrong, and it brought a number of difficult situations to the fore. Harry was nothing like my Swiss would-be client, although he did have a similar problem. He worked on an oil rig and consequently earned large amounts of money. He liked to take his R&R in the Land of Smiles, where he obviously became parted from his earnings rather rapidly. I took a call from him one afternoon, and agreed to wander down to meet him at the Silver Dollar Bar in Washington Square where we could have a chat about a little problem he had.

Like many of the Silver Dollar's clientele, Harry had been a regular patron for many years. Most of the Soi Washington bars trace their beginnings, or original owners, back to the days of the Vietnam War R&R, and the clients tend to be not the new-in-town, bargirl-hunting types, but more often than not those that have been there, done that, and are happy to talk about past conquests while steadily consuming Budweiser or Jack Daniels.

It was around 3 pm when I opened the door and entered the dimly lit, but (compared to the outside temperature) refreshingly cool Silver Dollar Bar. Young, good-looking bargirls know they have far more chance of making money in the Patpong or Nana complexes, and so it was an older, but nonetheless pleasant bargirl who poured me a JD and coke and pointed to a booth opposite the bar when I asked if Harry was around.

Harry was probably pushing fifty and obviously fond of a drink, with the initially reserved demeanour common to most guys spending time on oil rigs or in remote parts of the world. Perhaps he was just a deep thinker, brooding, but it was apparent that something was bothering him, so like any good interrogator, I introduced myself, shook hands, and then sat back enjoying the JD, and waited until he was ready to divulge what was on his mind.

Bit by bit, I got Harry's story. He told me he had been married to a Thai girl for about seven or eight years now and had bought her a nice apartment, not too far from where we were. He didn't stay there anymore, he said, as they were separated, and he understood there was now a younger German guy in the picture. "Mmmm," I thought, "a simple surveillance job, just to make sure Harry doesn't get totally screwed in a divorce proceeding, and that he gets a share of the apartment back." Wrong again.

"She can have the apartment," he said. "That's no problem. I'm not short of money; it's my boy I'm worried about."

Harry went on to say that the main reason he came to Bangkok these days was to see his son and to have a few drinks with some old expat mates. He accepted that as his wife was still young and he was not often around, it was quite on the cards for her to have an affair – and not too big a deal for him. What had happened was that the latest beau was talking about taking her and her son off to live in downtown Berlin. Harry didn't wish to travel halfway round the world to see his son, or even know if he would be able to see him. And, of course, he also preferred the scenery around the Silver Dollar's neighbourhood to gazing at the Brandenburg Tor!

Obviously, Harry had been a very good provider over the years. As he was somewhat of a loner, there was no one other than his former wife and son to benefit from his high earnings – except perhaps for a few Bangkok bars.

The lad had just turned four, he told me, and, in fact, was due to start at Bangkok's best International School kindergarten when the new term began in a week or two. Almost US$10,000 a year, Harry informed me. "But that's fine," he said. "I want him to have a good education and also to speak English." He noted my eyebrows rise appreciably when he mentioned the yearly fee. "I did call the kindergarten and speak to the principal," he told me, and it seemed that was the correct rate. But, he was assured, the care, and clientele, were all of the highest standard.

I chatted with Harry a bit longer, but it was hard to ascertain just what I could do. Obviously, he was not short of money. (Which, for some reason I could never figure out, was a condition that didn't normally apply to me!) I suggested therefore that we do some surveillance on his wife, see just what sort of care the child was getting, and also try to get some initial background on the Berlin beau. Harry was more than happy with this suggestion. In fact, most of my clients understood that they were totally in the dark regarding proceedings once they departed the Kingdom, and having a representative on hand that they could call on, or who could update them of goings-on, was usually quite a relief. It was a relief for my landlord, too, of course!

A week later, armed with a nice retainer from Harry, I set off early to locate his ex-wife's apartment, which was in a reasonable block of apartments on a small but pleasant *soi* off Soi Thonglor. There was a convenient street stall almost opposite where I was able to get a Coke poured into a plastic bag with some ice, and another bag with sliced pineapple, which set me back a whole 20 baht. I then sat down at a little plastic table to await young Simon heading off to pre-school. The school started at 8 am, and the kindergarten was 30 minutes away, so I had arrived shortly after seven. Yet, by 8 am, there was still no sign of Harry's pride and joy.

Whilst spending one's nights in air-conditioned bars surrounded by nubile young Thai girls is certainly most enjoyable, the hours sitting around in humid, smoggy Bangkok suburbs, sweating profusely and often waiting in vain for an appearance, does not fall into the same level of enjoyment. However, during my days as a private eye, the latter tended to take up far more hours than the former!

By 8:30, I had had enough, so I bade farewell to my food supplier and said I might see her again the next day. The following day, the same routine, and the only person getting anything positive out of the exercise was, again, the food seller. Not one to be discouraged, on day three, I was in for the long haul. If it took all day, I was going to wait until I managed to get a look at the former Mrs Harry in the flesh, and, hopefully, young Simon as well. Well, it didn't take the whole day fortunately, as it was a humid 38 degrees and I doubt I would have lasted that long. Just before 10 am, I saw the pair of them come down to the lobby and walk out, then head up the *soi*.

I didn't need to follow them far, just up a small side lane, and into a nondescript villa that had a small sign outside, in Thai, proclaiming "Pre-School Teaching, 10 am – 3 pm Monday to Friday, 500 baht per week." Why wasn't I surprised!

I noted down the contact number, then headed back to my apartment. Three early mornings and the heat of the day were getting to me: I needed an afternoon nap and a decent night out at one of the aforementioned bars to get things back to normal. Before dozing off and contemplating which venue I would honour with my presence that evening, I did call the pre-school. I was told that the teacher was very experienced, the wife of a local policeman in fact, and that no, at this stage there was no English included, but for an additional fee it could perhaps be arranged.

I was starting to take an active dislike to Harry's ex, who it seemed was indeed using their child as a means of parting my client from his hard-earned cash in any way she could. I sent a quick email updating Harry on his son's education, knowing he would be less than impressed, and saying that, in reality, there was not a lot we could do about it.

I knew that his wife was a frequent email user, so I asked Harry for the password of the email address he used to contact her, told him I needed it for 24 hours, and he could re-set it again after that. I then made a quick call to my computer wizard friend Jeremy and arranged to meet him in the After School Bar later that evening, and then it was siesta time. (I had developed the rather handy routine for a Bangkok night owl of having a regular afternoon siesta. I figured that as the key targets of many of my investigations, the cute young Thai girls, were generally doing likewise, I might as well join them!)

So it was an approaching dusk – or perhaps an unusually heavy smog – that greeted me when I peered through the curtains some hours later. A quick shower had me refreshed and ready for the night's activities. Jeremy, whom I had arranged to meet, was a rare find, a gem in fact for a struggling private eye. Now, I know how to turn a computer off and on, I even know how to find and scan all types of chatrooms, Matchmaker sites, and how to check an IP address, but that's about the limit of my IT expertise. Jeremy, on the other hand, was truly a computer whiz. But I'll tell you a little bit more about Jeremy and my relationship with him later.

Jeremy was in the "naughty-boys corner" when I walked into After School at around midnight, with Miss Yu-ee feeding him tequilas with her spare hand. They both gave me a big smile as I entered. "*Yu-ee, choke je-arh*," I called out, telling her in her native Khamen that she was having good luck, knowing full well she would be getting a decent tip plus plenty of tequilas out of Jeremy.

"No, not me lucky, you friend lucky," the young girl from Buriram shouted back.

By then, I was something of a regular at After School, where the girls believed I worked in the vague field of arranging visas for people! Anyway, on this occasion, it was more about business, at least as far as I was concerned. I extricated one rather large Jeremy from a very small Miss Yu-ee and signalled the girls to give us a break. I passed on the relevant email details I had from Harry, and briefly outlined the case, and the possible plight of Harry and his son. I dug into my wallet for a few thousand baht to give Jeremy for his time, but, great lad that he is, he waved that away.

"Just find out the current standing of that new barmaid," he said.

"You've been here too long," I told him. "You're already able to spot the fresh young girls on the scene." I didn't let on to Jeremy that I had already sourced that particular information: the baby-faced barmaid was in fact 32, and had three children back in her village to care for now that her husband had moved on.

As it was still relatively early and the After School Bar was somewhat small anyway, there were only a couple of other patrons in the place. So as I was up a few thousand baht thanks to Jeremy's benevolence, in a rare moment of extravagance, I beckoned Yu-ee over and told her to "ring the bell" – signifying that I was shouting the bar. This was greeted with great excitement in the bar, and, of course, it all helped build up the questionable image of what a great guy I really was.

But back to our story: Even allowing for the generous bell-ringer's tab, I figured I was still well in front. I went and got my own refill from the new barmaid, and mentioned to her that my friend Jeremy was even more *jai dee* than I. (*Jai dee* is usually translated as "good-hearted", although as far as bargirls are concerned, the term rather suggests someone who is a "soft touch".) What's more, I added, he was very interested in her. By this stage, smiles were beaming all over the place, and there was lots of clinking of glasses and shouts of "*Choke dee*!" (Good luck!); in other words, the camaraderie of a Bangkok bar at its best !

It was three days before Jeremy got back to me. Apparently, a certain barmaid had taken up all of his attention in the interim. However, I gathered that the six letters he mentioned (ZZZZZZ) referred to Harry's ex-wife's email and her password and not to his own need for more sleep. (Although he certainly sounded like he could use some additional sleep.) It's quite amazing, the simple passwords chosen by many of the people I investigated. Still, I was sure Harry would be pleased with the result, and that he was getting better value for his money from me than he was from what he was lavishing on his son's current education fund.

I went online and spent an hour or two browsing the estranged Mrs Harry's email, thankful that a trait of many Thai girls is not to delete mail. (I guess they think it's handy to have all correspondence on hand, just to remind themselves what they have actually said at times – or is that just my cynical beliefs surfacing again?)

There were a number of emails to various gentlemen with Western addresses, for the majority of whom, it seemed, contact had come via some of the many online matchmaker sites that she obviously belonged to. Of late, however, it was clear that the main man was certainly one Herr Rick Loppitz of Altenburg, Germany, and that the prospects of Harry's former wife and son heading Westward were indeed very real, whereas a certain David, from Brighton in the UK, seemed destined to be passed over. (Fortunately for David, I thought.)

I noted Herr Ricks email address, and put that to one side. I did wonder how he would react to an unsolicited email from an unknown Bangkok private eye. I would need to word it carefully, but in most cases, I found those involved in Thai intrigues at any level were happy to receive all kinds of information on mutual acquaintances residing in the Land of Smiles!

I gave the case some thought; foremost in my mind was the well-being of Harry's son, and in this respect, it was also a matter of taking the long view. I decided that before contacting Herr Rick, I would check out some facts and figures with the local German embassy. So the following day, I made a trip to Sathorn Road.

What I saw gave me a little jolt: it was perhaps the largest single gathering of obviously "night-working" Thai girls I had seen out anywhere during daylight hours! The fact that most of them seemed totally bored, and obviously would have preferred to be in their rooms asleep rather than waiting for visas or interviews, didn't seem to be registering on the infatuated males they were with, who were no doubt contemplating a home back in *Deutschland* with their *Liebchen*. Cynic that I am, I was sure the ladies were at the same time contemplating a new home for the family in Ban Nok (upcountry Thailand) or whether that month's payment from other various "sponsors" had arrived!

I had dealt with the German embassy a few times before, so I knew who to ask for, and by and large the German bureaucrats there were more helpful than their US or British counterparts; perhaps the fact that Koh Samui was often known as "Little Frankfurt" had something to do with it!

Jürgen motioned me into a side room a few moments after I had asked for my card to be presented to him.

As he was relatively young for a diplomat, I doubted Jürgen

was corruptible, but, like all of his kind, he was always keen to catch up on any local gossip, so I passed on a few titbits about one or two of his countrymen and then raised the question of Harry's son perhaps becoming a future German citizen. Jürgen agreed it could be a possibility, but assured me that for now, a three-month tourist visa was all that would be forthcoming. He made the necessary note, along with my contact details as the boy's father's representative.

The next step was to email the German boyfriend. As mentioned, I never knew how these third-party contacts would react, but by and large, I found most people I dealt with pretty reasonable, and keen for knowledge on their current lover. In this case, as expected, German common sense prevailed.

As was my style – or should I say, vindictive nature? – I didn't spare Herr Rick too many details. I told him I was acting for Harry; that is, Harry who had just paid nearly half a million baht for his son's education for the year and found the boy was instead attending a 500 baht-a-week cheap local establishment. I mentioned Harry's natural concern, adding that he did not want to lose contact with the lad and was worried he might end up in Altenburg, or – and yes, I just couldn't help myself – Brighton.

The reply from Rick was almost instantaneous. No questions about how I had his email address, but "what was this about Brighton?". Rick himself had been led to believe that the boy's father had died and left a poor, grieving wife struggling to bring up the lad as best she could!

I sent him back a copy of the transaction Harry had made to his ex-wife's account for school fees, assured him Harry was alive and well, then told him David of Brighton was also a "friend" of the lovely former Mrs Harry and that my contact in the German embassy would be closely monitoring any visa applications. Rick, sensible German that he was, then emailed me back asking for suggestions as to how to proceed, so I filled him in on the Thai P4P system, explained that this was basically the category his beloved fit into, and that he would be well-advised to keep to that sort of arrangement as far as she was concerned. Pay her for her time if you come to visit her; otherwise, put her, and her demands, out of your mind, I advised.

I then assured Rick that regardless of what she had threatened to do, when she learned a trip with Lufthansa was now unlikely, she would remain in contact – and be at the airport to meet him anytime her presence was requested! Standard Thai "P4P girl" practice was to never completely cut ties with a past sponsor.

Rick emailed me back a few times, thanking me for the advice, and advising me that things had gone exactly as I'd predicted. So, for the time being, crisis averted. The final step was to pay the lovely lady in question a visit.

I arranged for Sakdah, one of my Thai part-time helpers who ran a small travel agency but gave the impression of being a very serious and senior official, to accompany me. Most Asians are aware that serious fraud officers, and other high-ranking enforcement people, always go about in plainclothes, so they often have more respect for them than the uniformed kind. We were let into a typical Thai apartment, clean and tidy, with a large photo of King Rama V on the wall – although none of Harry that I could see!

I walked straight over to a small coffee table and laid down a copy of the school fee transaction Harry had made, a photo of her and her son coming out of the nearby Thai pre-school, as well as an admissions application for the high-priced kindergarten.

"I am investigating a fraud charge," I told her in Thai, and nodded towards Sakdah, who stood there with an official-looking notebook in his hand.

"My friends in the American and German embassies are asking questions about you," I told her, and added that local people were wondering if she was fit to take care of her son!

Anger, shock, amazement registered in her face, all at the one time. I knew better than to try and argue or reason with a Thai woman. I simply held up a hand to silence her and said, "Have the boy enrolled in the correct school tomorrow and no further action will be taken. Also see that he is ALWAYS available to meet his father when requested."

"By the way," I added as I headed for the door, "neither the German nor British embassy intend to grant you a visa." Well, yes, I was taking liberties, but as far as I was concerned, she had well overstepped the mark in regards to the boy's education and, consequently, his possible future. Perhaps the reality, or shock, of what she had done or been discovered doing sunk in, as there was no sound or attempted explanation from her. I motioned for Sakdah to exit, and we quickly left the building before she thought to ask for some ID, or even ask a few relevant questions of us. My idea had been to shock her into doing the right thing; considering that she was from a fairly humble background, I thought it had a good chance of working.

I then contacted Harry, and we discussed all that had happened. He understood that in future, he would be best off making any such payments directly to the school. As I gather, he did have to slightly "replenish" the pre-school fund, but I was able to report a week or two later that the boy was indeed attending the much higher-class establishment.

Of course, not all cases get so neatly finalized. One other case that comes to mind started with an email I received from a former US Army soldier who had been diagnosed with terminal cancer.

He had been in Bangkok some 30 years earlier and had an affair with a Thai girl. The girl had become pregnant, he had covered initial expenses, but then returned to the States and had had no further contact.

He forwarded me an address, and a Thai family name, and although I was able to locate the house, there was no knowledge of the woman or child. There was little more I could do, but I pointed out that once a Thai woman has crossed what is quite a substantial line, to have an affair with a *farang* or foreigner, they will in most cases continue down that path. (Whether this is because they are then shunned by Thai men, or genuinely do wish to have a Western husband, depends on the particular woman involved.) Quite possibly, I suggested, this ex-GI's former girlfriend and child had ended up living a comfortable life in a foreign country. I never did hear back from him, so that was one more case that slid into the unsolved basket.

A postscript: Certainly cases involving children, such as maintenance deals, visitation rights and DNA tests, did come our way from time to time. This was especially true for children of mixed heritage. As you can imagine, when the parents have gone their separate ways, and that extends to separate continents, it can make things especially stressful or difficult for all concerned.

Obviously, there is no easy answer. However I would like to point out that, from a personal viewpoint, Thai women, regardless of their background or upbringing, tend to make wonderful mothers. Indeed, in more cases than not, I have seen the birth of a Thai-Western child strongly cement a relationship.

Oh yes, I had promised to explain how computer whiz Jeremy and I had come to such a pleasant working relationship. It seems that Jeremy had developed some arcane piece of software a few years back and received a very, very large payout from some Silicon Valley outfit. He had then flown to Bangkok to meet up with a "movie star" he had met online, who hadn't looked quite so angelic or pale-skinned in the flesh. (Amazing what the photo shops in the cut-rate Marboonkrong shopping complex can do to enhance pictures.) However, as Jeremy was hardly movie star material himself (unless you were casting an overweight, dishevelled nerd), he didn't notice. He was ecstatic just to have a girlfriend of any type, let alone a young and relatively good-looking one. She was also very understanding and let Jeremy have lots of time to himself at night to do his computer browsing, which is how he stumbled across a local chat site where some kind soul had had a nice word to say about TPE.

I had met Jeremy at a nearby Starbucks, and soon had his life story, and also a look at a handful of pictures of his beloved, who I instantly knew was not, as she had informed him, going home at night to care for her sick grandmother.

I advised him to invest in a new mobile phone for Miss Du and, before giving it to her, to install a very handy system we had access to. Jeremy had insisted on paying me a full day's rate for our little chat and advice, so, of course, I told him to call me anytime he had a problem. I hadn't expected that to be the same evening, but he called me around 10 pm, most apologetic about the hour.

"That's okay," I had told him. I was just starting out on my nightly rounds, which meant going to my regular footpath venue, on Soi 13, sitting on a plastic stool and eating satay chicken washed down with *Sangthip*, a cheap Thai rice whisky popular with those who can't afford Johnny Black.

It was too early for the local talent parade to start passing my prime spot, strategically situated between the Soi Cowboy and Nana entertainment plazas, so I told him I would be at the Emporium Suites shortly, and a five-minute motorcycle taxi ride had me at his trendy abode.

I learnt how excited Du had been with her new phone, and how, as normal, she had left the apartment a couple of hours earlier, so as to get home before it got late and Grandma got worried. Shortly thereafter, Jeremy had logged onto the site our spyware connected to, which very conveniently records all text messages sent and received by that phone. There had been plenty of action, although most of it was in Thai script. I wouldn't say I'm foolproof in reading Thai, but I do get by okay. In any case, with this one, it was pretty hard to mistake the CM2!

Miss Du had apparently decided to leave her sick grandmother on her own for the evening whilst she visited a popular nightclub and well-known pick-up joint called CM Square. I told Jeremy it might be best if I went over there to follow up and had hardly been able to mention that a few expenses might be incurred before he had thrust five 1000 baht notes in my hand. Hence, soon thereafter, I had happily upgraded my plastic stool on the footpath in the humid, smog-laden Bangkok air for a padded one at the delightfully air-cooled CM Square nightclub.

Spotting a reasonable-looking Thai girl, late twenties, with long black hair and probably dressed in trendy Levis with a small, tight-fitting T-shirt in CM Square was as easy as finding a needle in a haystack. However, as per usual, I had asked Jeremy to detail any recent jewellery he had bought his lady, as it was fairly certain this would be flashed for all and sundry to see. Sure enough, an hour and three JD-and-Cokes later, an overlarge gold bracelet with dangling hearts confirmed that I had located the lovely Miss Du.

She was with three friends, and it was quite obvious who was paying. Indirectly, of course, it was poor Jeremy! In any group of trendy Thai girls, there always seems to be least one girl who currently has a sponsor and is able to pay the taxi and entrance fees, not to mention a round or two of drinks. Pay, that is, until one of the many circling "sprats" – who mistakenly believe they are sharks – gets pulled into the net to take over the night's payments.

Suffice it to say, Miss Du was very much a player. I didn't even need to resort to using one of my younger, better-looking associates to effect a sting. A few days later, I had Jeremy perched up in the balcony of the Marriott Hotel, seeing his beloved, ostensibly at home caring for Grandma, saunter in to meet up with a guy she believed to be a very wealthy and famous Australian movie producer, who in reality was a struggling Kiwi private eye. As a result, Ms Du lost a very good sponsor, and I gained an invaluable ally in the IT field.

To say invaluable was, in fact, doing Jeremy a disservice: In most cases, all he needed was an email address, and preferably the email address of a contact known to the person you were checking on, and there was little he couldn't find out about the unsuspecting person's on-line activities.

Of course, the big plus for struggling TPE was that Jeremy was very rich and loved being involved. Hence, a few drinks at a – yes, I admit it – "sleazy" bar and getting me to give a quick assessment of his possible night's companion was more than enough payment for him. As you can see from the above story concerning Harry and his son.

HORSES FOR COURSES

"There is no secret so close
as that between a rider and his horse."
Robert Smith Surtees

Whilst there have been a number of "would-be" or quasi-investigation agencies set up by Westerners following my early days as a private eye in the mid-1990s, these firms typically struggle for credibility, as they are often run by astute enforcement people who either don't live full-time in the Kingdom or else do not speak the language. Others have been run locally, but just don't have those local contacts required in certain areas who can at times prove to be of great assistance.

There are, however, numerous very professional Thai investigation companies operating, and it was always my rule, where applicable, to leave the investigating of Thais to them. Yes, it is true that some of the less scrupulous Thai companies have been known to take their "findings" to the person being investigated and, for a hefty fee, agree to submit an altered report to the actual client. But, after all, "TIT" (or "This Is Thailand"), as we tend to say.

However, in this one particular case that I recall, I did agree to meet and hear the obviously Western-educated Thai guy who rang me up one Monday morning. The reason for the call was that he had looked into my background, and as the case revolved around racehorses, he felt I might be just the right person for the job.

From time to time, there were articles written about my business and myself in various magazines around Asia, so I guess it wasn't too difficult to find out that my real introduction to Asian peoples back in the 1980s had been as a part-time horse trader. Of course, I had supplemented that income as a hotel manager over the years before ending up founding, almost by accident, Thai Private Eye. That had happened when the owners of the largest hotel in Thailand's Northeast at the time had to leave the country in a hurry, and in their haste left their Western manager (yours truly) jobless, but with a very good understanding of Thai, Khamen, the local ways and culture, as well as with many influential contacts throughout the Kingdom.

I told my caller, who said his name was Lek, that for security reasons, I would not meet him at my office. (Which at that time happened to be my spare room and which was also just then occupied by a rather large Kiwi friend and a very small Thai bargirl). Instead, we agreed to meet at a Starbucks near Lek's Silom office.

I had some familiarity with the Thai thoroughbred and racing industry, and knew it was very corrupt; at least in those days, it was. However, along with having a Mercedes-Benz, owing a racehorse was a sign of great "face" amongst many Asian people, and in that respect, Thais were certainly no different.

It was a rule of the Kingdom that horses had to be bred there to be allowed to race at the two city racetracks where racing was held every Sunday. These particular horses traced directly back to Mongolian ponies and tended to be rather small compared to Western thoroughbreds.

With the Thai penchant for loopholes, those in power (not to mention any names, but it's worth noting that both the Thai army and police have cavalry units) came up with the idea of importing stallions or even broodmares in foal, usually from New Zealand or Australia.

By breeding these horses with local mares, they had a foal born within the Kingdom that could therefore be officially registered to race, but which actually had a lot more "blue blood" running through its veins and which was also typically bigger and faster than local pure-breds.

One very astute and influential Thai noted that while the New Zealand or Australian horses, like those bred in Thailand itself, were branded with a number burnt into the shoulder when young, as cattle are branded, horses from the USA had a "clean" shoulder. American racehorses instead had a lip tattoo performed on them as registration, along with blood and DNA tests.

A new plan was devised to import horses directly from Hollywood Park, then have the brands of a rather slow Thai racehorse put on the shoulder, and – hey, presto – you had developed a new horse that could suddenly cover the 1,200 meters of most Thai races about six or seven seconds faster then the typical Thai-bred thoroughbred. And that worked out to around 100 meters faster than its namesake could travel that track!

Lek hailed from a wealthy Thai family. His father was in electronics, he told me, as we chatted over a coffee. He was in his mid-thirties, dressed immaculately, and exuded that air of confidence one has when surrounded by wealth in what is basically a poor country. He said he had studied in Sydney for some time, although as we talked mainly horses, it was evident most of his study had been done at Royal Randwick.

At some point, Lek had decided to get involved in the local racing industry, so he approached a very high-profile Thai stud and training complex. As is often the case in Thailand, he was given the opportunity of buying a well-bred foal at a stage when the foal was still in the womb. But he was shown veterinary reports and also an ultra-scan confirming that the mare was carrying a healthy foal. The mare, he was assured, had been bred in Australia and had a heritage that went back to the famed Star Kingdom, one of the greatest sires to stand in the Southern Hemisphere. The mare duly foaled, and Lek was the proud owner of a nice, healthy colt.

As is usually the case, the foal remained at the stud, which was also a training complex. At around 18 months of age, it began its education. All was fine, it seemed; Lek was paying hefty monthly training and feed bills, but this was irrelevant as it was just a matter of time before the horse was mature enough to race, and then, considering his breeding, he would certainly be a winner, perhaps even the winner of the prestigious King's Cup one day.

Once horses turn two, they are generally developed enough to race. The practice in Thailand is that they are then taken onto the racetrack, where they first have to pass what by Western standards would be a rather moderate qualifying time. Covering 1,000 meters in around 1 minute, 6 seconds is the usual requirement, a good six or seven seconds slower than the average Australian or New Zealand thoroughbred would usually run that distance.

This is where the problem, or in Lek's case, doubts had begun. Despite three attempts so far, the horse had been unable to break the qualifying time. Not only was he not winning any races, he was not even fast enough to be allowed to race!

The trainer had given various reasons – immaturity, unsuitable track conditions, et cetera – for the horse's poor showings. Lek, however, was beginning to think otherwise. He wondered if the so-called Australian-bred pony he had paid over a million baht for was, in fact, from the famous Star Kingdom line at all. Had a switch taken place at some stage?

My brief, then, was to somehow confirm the breeding or bloodlines of his expensive would-be champion, which it seemed couldn't run out of sight on a dark night. Many people, myself included, just don't run fast; horses are the same. However, assuming that the horse was fit and healthy, which I would need to confirm, and it was a thoroughbred with bloodlines as indicated, it should certainly have been able to at least break the qualifying time.

I asked Lek for all the paperwork, photos, copies of brands that he had, of both the foal and its alleged parents, along, of course, with a nice, hefty retainer. He had all the relevant papers on hand, so I told him I would get on the job immediately and get in contact with my informed parties in Australia. Typically of the Thai attitude in such a situation, this wasn't so much about the money, as about the loss of face involved in owning a supposedly well-bred horse that was very slow!

I saved myself a host of international calls and accessed the Australian thoroughbred stud book online. With the details and brands Lek had given me, I was able to see that the dam, or alleged mother, of his horse had indeed been shipped to Thailand a couple of years previously, and, at that time, she had indeed been covered by a nondescript stallion that was a somewhat poor relation of the mighty Star Kingdom. This meant that the paperwork was correct; well, correct to a point. The most important question: was the resulting foal, which had cost Lek a million baht, the actual horse that he was now the not-quite-so proud owner of? (By my calculations, the price he paid was about five times the cost of buying the mare in Australia, in foal, and having her shipped to Thailand.)

I spent a couple of days hatching out a plan. Large amounts of money and influential people were all involved here, so I needed to get it right. We met at Starbucks the following Monday.

What we needed to do, I told him, was to go and see the horse and covertly take a blood sample, as well as some hair from the horse's mane, which could then confirm its DNA. The samples would have to be sent to Australia, the blood would need to be frozen, all a rather expensive undertaking, but the only way to make certain confirmation. Lek promptly pulled a large wad of 1,000-baht notes out of his designer jacket. "Just to keep you going," he said.

We decided to travel up to the horse farm the following Sunday. As Sunday is race day in Bangkok, there would be few people around, and certainly not the trainer or the farm's owner.

Rather than snoop around in the dark, as I have an aversion to underfed Thai dogs and snakes, I had decided the best plan was for Lek to drive a friend and me to the property, which was near Chonburi, about 50 kilometres outside Bangkok. As it was along the route to Pattaya, we would use the cover story that he was taking some *farang* friends to the beach resort, and, while on the way, was just calling in to see his horse. I informed Lek that I had also arranged for a photographer to come with us, and he would film any evidence that we might need.

I could tell he was impressed by that move, and I made a mental note to add "photographer's fee" to the final bill. About time my rather large Kiwi houseguest Phil (whom I had recruited to be our photographer) gave those bargirls a day off and made himself useful, I thought. Plus, Phil was a rather solid, menacing-looking bloke. Not that I envisaged any problems, but he would be rather handy backup if things went awry.

Lek picked us up in a silver Mercedes at midday. I don't at all doubt the statistic someone once told me that there are more Mercedes-Benzes in Bangkok than in Berlin, part of the Thai "face" thing. If you have money, you need to show it. Which, of course, was also part of the reason for Lek's horse problem in the first place.

Being a Sunday, for once the traffic was reasonably light, and we headed out through Rhamkhamheng and onto the freeway to Pattaya. A bit of a shudder went up my spine as we passed through the tollway, the very one I had used to escape a couple of gun-wielding motorcyclists some months earlier, when, innocently staking out a case of infidelity, I had stumbled across a drug distribution centre. (See *Confessions of a Bangkok Private Eye* , "The case of the double-crossed Dutchman".)

The fact that Chonburi, where we were going, was notorious for producing the Kingdom's top "hit-men" did little to calm my fears, although Phil suggested that my shakes perhaps had a lot more to do with the two bottles of Jack Daniels we had finished off at the Dance Fever nightclub the previous evening.

We drove past a number of golf courses, then down a side road, before coming to an expansive post and railed property that was one of the area's more prominent thoroughbred horse breeding and training centres.

As we suspected, there was little sign of life early on a Sunday afternoon; most staff were either at the races or asleep. Phil and I got out of the car and went over to look at a small sandy training track and to check that the video camera was operating, while Lek ambled over to the staff quarters to see if he could rouse someone.

Lek appeared a few moments later with a stable hand who had obviously consumed a fair bit more alcohol than Phil and I the previous night. But the fellow was nonetheless the usual affable and willing helper in such circumstances – that is, when a rich owner was around – and he assumed a decent tip would most likely be forthcoming.

The stable boy picked up a head collar and lead, and headed off down a laneway, returning a few minutes later with a somewhat frisky, bay-coloured horse jig-jogging along beside him.

Even at first glance, I had grave doubts there was any of Star

Kingdom's blue blood in those veins. A nice enough horse, and in not bad condition, but he had a rounded or Roman nose and not the fine, dish-shaped head of an aristocratic thoroughbred.

Of course, I had grown up in what is called the Kentucky of the Southern Hemisphere, a small town in New Zealand where thoroughbreds far outnumbered people, and I figured the stud owners felt they'd be fairly safe in assuming no Thai client would have such an eye.

The stable worker tied the horse up in a stall, and I mentioned to Lek that perhaps the horse could have a quick brush before we took some pictures. He pulled a 500 baht note out of his top pocket, palmed it to the boy, and asked him in to get a brush. As the boy headed off to the tack room, I told Phil to switch on the video cam and make sure he focused on the horse's brands, with no more of me in the shot than my hands.

I pulled out a small syringe, pressed on the horse's jugular vein, and, as it rose, drained off a small amount of blood, then pulled some strands of hair out of the horse's mane: two foolproof methods of confirming DNA. I saw the boy returning with the brushes, so I sauntered back towards Lek's car, mentioning it was too hot for me.

I then got a collection vial containing anti-coagulant out of the glove box, squirted the blood sample in, marked and sealed it, and placed the hair sample in an envelope. Both samples then went into a specially padded bag addressed to the Australian horse registrar in Sydney. Lek and Phil returned a few moments later, we drove out of the farm, and, instead of driving on towards Pattaya, headed back to Bangkok, making a short stop along the way at a freight-forwarding office.

Within a week, I had confirmation of what I had suspected: there was no Star Kingdom DNA in the samples, and it was without doubt that the horse's pedigree was not as officially listed.

I had made it pretty clear to Lek that whilst I would collect the evidence, I didn't want to be involved further, another reason I had told Phil to include only my hands in his frame. The stud owners were very, and I mean VERY, well-connected, and even allowing for the hefty fee Lek was paying, I didn't want to be the one to tell them they had perhaps made a mistake in regards to his horse's parentage.

A few days later, I met up with Lek again, handed him the reply from the Australian authorities, along with the video clip, and pocketed the large envelope he handed me. I told him to be careful as to how and where he presented his evidence and to be sure my name did not get a mention. I then added that I would, however, certainly be interested in the outcome.

I was somewhat relieved to get a call from him the following week; I had been looking over my shoulder even more than usual since that sample-collecting escapade. Apparently, the stud owner had apologized profusely and come up with the usual Thai face-saving answer. "Obviously one he had in store for such an occasion" was my reaction ... but remember, I am a cynical son of a bitch!

This was the pained explanation: Lek had, you'll remember, paid the very hefty fee for his horse whilst it was still a foetus. By some stroke of terrible misfortune, his foal had actually been born dead. The stud owner told Lek that he himself had been overseas at the time, and the staff who had overseen the foaling had been too frightened to tell him of the tragedy. Another mare had foaled around the same time, so to cover up this sad event, they, the staff members, had done a swap.

The owner told Lek how devastated he had been to find this out, and that he had immediately sacked all those involved. He also mentioned that under the stud's agreement, if a foal was born dead, you did, sadly lose your stake. In this case, however, as he was so embarrassed by the chain of events, he would refund Lek's money and simply request that Lek keep the whole affair quiet.

Lek had been happy enough with the outcome, and assured me that if not for my help, he never would have got anything back. He had had enough of the horse-racing scene for now, he told me, and was instead going to invest in a racing yacht!

For my part, I wasn't quite so convinced about that so convenient explanation. I told you I was cynical.

I took to buying the weekly Thai racing guide, and a few months later, I noticed the stud in question had a very ordinary bred 2-year-old colt making its debut at the Bangkok track. I joined the throngs on Henri Dunant Avenue heading for the track, the month's rent money in my pocket. I didn't have to wait long: the 2-year-old's race was the first one on the day's card.

A showy black colt with a white blaze, characteristic of many Star Kingdom horses, was among those parading for the event, and this one even turned my way and gave me a nod of his head. The landlord never really had any worries: the horse went straight to the front and increased its lead. The rent was good for the next six months, and a number of my local female acquaintances found out that I wasn't quite so *kee-neo* after all.

(*Kee-neo* is the word often used by Thai working girls to describe a customer they see as being stingy or tight with his money. I tend to believe it's actually someone who is quite astute!)

IN THE WAKE OF THE KILLER WAVES

*"I don't mind dying – I just don't want
to be there when it happens."*
Woody Allen

The events that shocked the world on December 26th, 2004 were indeed horrific.

However, for those actually involved, or based at the time in Phuket or Koh Phi Phi as some of our staff were, they were obviously far worse. These colleagues were confronted daily by distraught or grieving families and faced particularly stressful situations on all fronts.

One thing that especially saddened me was the many "unknowns" who disappeared on that fateful day – the many itinerant traders one sees at tourist or holiday resorts all over Thailand. These included peanut sellers who may have fled across the border from Burma, trying to eke out a better living for their families; those from Thailand's poor northeast, who may have left behind arid farmland to cook food at street stalls; and yes, even those working in prostitution, who were no longer young or assured of clients. All these types, along with the drunk, drugged and disorderly, would more often than not sleep on the beach or under a nearby palm. They were of no fixed abode, short on friends, and perhaps long out of contact with family. Many of these people were never seen or heard from again.

Thai Private Eye has several operatives based in Phuket, and I am proud of the fact that during this difficult time, we were amongst the first to offer humanitarian aid and to assist the local authorities in any manner that we could. Obviously, in the aftermath of the tsunami, we did get called upon to perform an investigative role. One rather intriguing case that I personally looked into did not come to my notice until quite some time after the actual tsunami.

I was approached by May, a very well-educated, attractive Thai woman in her mid-thirties.

She told me that a mutual friend had recommended me. In this case, it involved someone who is, I must admit, a rare breed in my circle of friends: that is, another Thai woman who was likewise from a very well-educated and respected Thai family.

May began by filling me in on some of her background. She had, like her brothers, attended medical school, and whilst they had gone on to become doctors, she had ventured into the beautician business. There had been an affair with a Thai doctor, but like many successful Thai men surrounded by opportunity, he had proven to be *jow shu* (a playboy)

May had then immersed herself in her work and, in fact, was at the forefront of various new techniques in the cosmetic world. She had an idea of maybe opening a chain of specialized clinics. However, although her family was well-off, they were perhaps not quite that affluent. It was around that time that she had met Rodney. The quintessential British expat, he oozed charm, money and breeding, all assets that appealed greatly to an upper-class Thai woman such as May.

They had met in Phuket, where May operated a clinic, at the high point of the resort's social calendar, the Royal Regatta. Rodney was, in fact, the owner of one of the larger yachts moored at the local Yacht Club. He also owned a villa nearby that he used when he was in Phuket. Whilst perhaps not a match made in heaven, it was nonetheless a very compatible coupling. May was very much at home in the high society circles Rodney moved in, and for his part, he had an attractive and well-respected partner.

Over the next few years, May had two children with Rodney; nannies, housekeepers, and, later, private schools were, of course, no problem for this high-powered couple. Rodney spent much of his time overseas, as he had offices in Spain and the Cayman Islands. As far as May was aware, her significant other was involved in international real estate. But, as is often the case with

Thai women, she did not ask too many questions and was not totally sure of just what he actually did.

May knew, however, that he was very rich: he provided her with whatever she or their children needed, and he allowed her plenty of space to continue with her interest in the cosmetic world. In pursuing these interests, May moved regularly between her Bangkok home and clinic, her Phuket clinic and their villa. By and large, all was well in her life.

Towards the end of 2004, Rodney's visits to Thailand became far less frequent. However, he had assured May he would be there for Christmas and New Year. True to his word, Rodney had flown into Bangkok a day or two before Christmas and had caught up with his wife and family, although to May, it was obvious they were drifting apart. Rodney said he wanted to catch up with some friends in Phuket, so he flew south, and May was to travel down with the children a few days later so they could spend New Year together. That was the last time she or her children ever saw him.

Unable to contact him by phone, with the whole region in turmoil, May had gone south as soon as she could. The villa was still standing, but only just: it was no longer inhabitable. As to Rodney, there was no sign whatsoever. She spent a rather traumatic few weeks checking unidentified bodies that had been recovered, but none of them was Rodney.

She tried to contact the few members of his family she knew or had heard about and received either no answer, a wrong number, or no comment. The British embassy took notes, but little else.

She stayed on in Phuket for six months. A small payment from the Thai government, as a partial compensation for loss of home, did not go far, and the land eventually reverted to the Thai state. Private school, nanny and living expenses soon depleted the bank accounts, whilst tourists or locals in need of beauty treatment were no longer plentiful. Finally, May had to leave Phuket, resigned to the fact her husband was probably dead, and return to her family home in Bangkok.

She knew Rodney was rich and assumed some provision would have been made for her and the children, but she had limited knowledge of his private affairs, and all enquiries she made quickly hit a brick wall. It was frustrating, but in true Thai manner, she learned to accept adversity, and not to question authority. She accepted her lot, conceded that the good times were over and that now she had to struggle, work hard, and try to raise and educate her children as best she could. Certainly, it would not be too hard for them, as her family was wealthy and she was again in demand in the beautician field. So gradually the past and the horror of what had happened at Phuket faded, and she moved on with her life.

Part and parcel of Thai life are regular visits to a fortune teller, or *mor dhu*, as they are known locally. From the humble bargirl to the Kingdom's leading politicians, all will make regular trips to those they believe are the more astute amongst the soothsayers, especially if some major change to their circumstances seems "on the cards", so to speak. They often make important decisions based on the *mor dhu*'s recommendations.

May was no different, and although not as firm a believer in fortune-telling as many, she did make the occasional visit. On one such visit, something stuck in her mind: the *mor dhu* had repeated that "your husband has left you." Perhaps that was the catalyst, along with that suggestion from our mutual friend that she really should look into any possible inheritance for her children.

There certainly seemed to be a few strange twists and turns to her tale. For instance, why Rodney's relatives would not at least be in touch seemed surprising, although I figured it was also quite likely, considering his constant travelling, that Rodney perhaps still had a wife back in the UK, and that his Thai family was something of a secret. It certainly wouldn't be the first time I had encountered that scenario.

I asked her to find all the names and paperwork relating to her husband she could, and she suggested I call around to her home the following evening when she would be able to show me everything that could be relevant. No doubt at all, May would have been a stunner in her younger days, and unlike a lot of Thai women, she was ageing particularly well, probably much better than me, I thought! So I told her I looked forward to seeing her again.

The three-storey townhouse was in a modern block at

Bangna. I often enjoyed travelling out to the suburbs, where a Westerner was a rarity and you got a far better perspective of how the majority of Bangkok's ten million inhabitants go about their daily lives.

The air-conditioned home and May's lingering perfume (Fendi, I suspected) together provided a

welcoming greeting as I stepped inside. I wondered if the perfume was for my benefit; certainly, the lovely, well-educated, successful and hard-working May would be a step up from my usual female acquaintances – although, upon further reflection, I'd have to say she'd be perhaps a step too far!

May took out a large manila folder that contained various papers, photos, and documentation, so I spent some time identifying various people in pictures and getting what information I could about her somewhat shady (or at least, low-profile) husband's past. One did not usually spend so much time away from one's family, especially if your wife was a gem such as May. For that matter, one usually didn't have an office on the Cayman Islands without having something to hide, I figured.

An hour later, armed with the manila folder, a few pages of notes in my trusty notebook, and a fond farewell, I was in a taxi and heading back to my apartment to start some research into the mysterious Rodney. I was unsure as to just whether the delightful May needed some physical consoling along with my professional help. But knowing Thais and the class system that operates there as well I do, the realist in me understood that her manner was that of the normal, well brought-up, polite and affable Thai woman and that my focus would have to remain fairly much on the missing husband rather than his wife!

As our Phuket office had worked closely with local police and government departments involved in the tsunami disaster, I did have a number of contacts I could easily get in touch with, but neither they nor the British embassy had any knowledge of Rodney's demise. As May had done, I tried to contact the members of her husband's family she knew of, but in most cases, the numbers were old or had changed, or else I got a short "I have no idea what happened to him."

By this time, over two years had passed since the tsunami, and although, as I mentioned, many itinerant workers may have been lost without a trace, it became increasingly obvious to me that someone who was British and wealthy would not have died in that disaster with absolutely no recognition, death notice, or at least a remembrance service. I felt the answers lay in the UK, more than likely in the form of another family, or perhaps a demanding wife that May had been blissfully unaware of. Unfortunately, May's budget would not cover a trip to "Old Blighty", so I continued to work mainly through the documentation and papers she had provided me with.

Buried somewhere in all this was an old letter from the lovely people at Royal Orchid, the frequent- flyer arm of Thai Airways.

Having contacts within major airlines is, of course, imperative in the private eye business. Admittedly, tapping such contacts is perhaps not ethical ... but hey, we are talking about Thailand, and fortunately, as far as I was concerned, people in the region were far more influenced by money than by things like privacy laws!

The following day I made a trip down Vipharvadi-Rangsit to the Thai Airways head office, and went to find Frank. Frank was conveniently in his office and at his computer terminal, although I noted it was on Ladbrokes.com rather than on anything connected with the airline!

Frank and I discussed the relative merits of Arsenal and Manchester United for a few minutes before I slipped him an envelope containing a few thousand baht and Rodney's frequent flyer number written on the outside. "You want print-out, Khun Warren?" he asked.

A few minutes later I was in a taxi, heading back to my apartment with full details of Rodney's flights over the past five years folded up in my shirt pocket, along with an assurance that Arsenal would win the Premiership that year. (Man U actually took the title.)

Rodney certainly had racked up the miles; he was a Gold Card member, and always flew business class. Bangkok, Heathrow and the Caymans featured prominently, particularly in the earlier days. However, it was when I got to the last page that I did a double-take: Rodney had flown Lufthansa to Malaga on the Costa del Sol just three weeks earlier! Thanks to German efficiency, and an airline co-op deal known as the Star Alliance, the good people at Lufthansa had transferred his air points to his Thai Airways card.

Now either someone was using Rodney's ID or credit card, or Rodney himself had changed his Thai *te ruk* (Thai term of affection, meaning "my love" or "my darling") for a Spanish senorita. In view of the heightened security arrangements at airports these days, I clearly opted for the latter explanation.

As transnational crime becomes perhaps the major problem facing enforcement agencies worldwide, co-operation amongst various agencies, including Interpol obviously, is becoming increasingly important. Unfortunately for a struggling Bangkok private eye, however, access to these types of files and the departments involved is not as easy as it is to many other organizations within the Kingdom. I thought that perhaps May should go to the local fraud office, and from there the international, inter-agency information that we wanted might become available. But working through those official channels is a very slow and drawn-out process, and May's attitude was that in her mind, Rodney was dead and gone, and that's how she wanted it to stay. The notion that, not so much she herself, but the couple's children had been abandoned by their father was just something she couldn't, or didn't want to, contemplate.

So although I had just about confirmed that he was indeed still alive, and she had asked me to dig up a little more information as to the reasons for his disappearance, she was not keen to get involved with Interpol or to make too big a fuss. This, by the way, is fairly much the Thai attitude in such cases. I had a good look through the wide range of contacts and clients I had built up over the years, and there were one or two in fairly strategic positions of law enforcement that I was able to call on to look a little further into this mystery man.

What I was finally able to put together was that Rodney had operated an international real estate business that seemed to specialize in selling overpriced properties to the rich and gullible.

It also seemed that selling the same property to two or three clients was not an unknown practice in this field, and, of course, beachfront villas in places like Phuket had also been sold to Western clients blissfully unaware that in Thailand not only are foreigners unable to buy land, but they cannot even buy a home.

(Thai law states that land is owned by the King, although often that land is on a 100-year lease. In true Thai style, there is a loophole regarding ownership of a dwelling: provided that an apartment or condominium block is 60% Thai-owned, single units within that structure may be owned by foreigners, but they cannot own a stand-alone dwelling.)

The Internet being what it is, with chat rooms and the like, disgruntled clients tend to communicate with each other.

Consequently, news of some of the companies Rodney was associated with, and their dubious dealings, had begun to surface. A number of lawsuits were pending, Interpol had indeed been alerted, some bank accounts had been frozen, and bankruptcy *cum* incarceration was looming large for Rodney. Then, out of the blue, the tsunami had not only given him a chance to escape, but also to cover up some of the very suspect deals he was currently involved in regarding the sale of Phuket villas.

In the turmoil surrounding the tsunami and its aftermath, it had been rather simple to pick up a friend's passport and jump on a bus to Penang in Malaysia. From there, with enough money, boarding a ship bound for almost any part of the world would not have been not too difficult either. As Rodney had family members in the UK who were also involved in the land deal scams, they had covered up for him and, of course, were sworn to complete secrecy.

Just how a man could, overnight, disassociate himself from his own children is something that neither May not I could ever figure out; nonetheless, that was the path Rodney had chosen.

For her part, May was deeply shocked by the turn of events, but decided to keep to her original belief, that her husband was lost in the tsunami. She did, however, decide to take a leaf from his book in one respect and accept an offer to transfer her beautician skills abroad: she has now relocated her family and likewise started a new life. In her case, thankfully, it is legal and successful. More, unlike her "late husband" Rodney, she doesn't have to look over her shoulder day and night.

THE PILGRIM'S PROGRESS

"Wherever we may come alive,
that is the area in which we are spiritual."
Brother David Steindl-Rast

We, of course, get a steady stream of requests from people who have lost contact with friends or family. These lost individuals are often young adults on the Big OE, or overseas experience, who have managed to get themselves waylaid somewhere around Southeast Asia. Koh Pang Nan is a popular haunt for such wide-eyed travellers. One reason perhaps: during the famed monthly full-moon parties, it is far easier to find a wandering beach vendor selling your particular drug of choice than it is to find one selling food or drink! Consequently, losing track of time, or failing to call home, is not all that uncommon.

In one of these cases, Beth and Harry from downtown Saskatoon, Canada had contacted me, as they were worried about their son Joel, especially after the murderous tsunami of December 2004. Following the usual background info and pictures, I determined that Joel, who had recently graduated from Saskatchewan University, was unlikely to make the local hockey team or become a star quarterback. I could well imagine that for this young man, a rather slight, bespectacled lad, many sights throughout the Asian region would have indeed been real eye-openers for him.

The last contact Beth and Harry had received was an email from an Internet café in Ho Chi Minh two weeks previously. Joel had said he was going to head across Laos to Thailand, and possibly return home after spending some time in Bangkok. Although it was some months after the disaster, I still had to assure them that his travel plans were very much inland, and the chances of a tsunami sailing up the Mekong were rather remote.

The easiest method of getting through Laos to Bangkok from Vietnam would be to go via Vientiane, and then across the Friendship Bridge at Nong Khai, straight down the main highway to the City of Angels, as Bangkok is known. Nevertheless, backpackers tend to pick up maps, look at the shortest route rather than the easiest and head that way.

I had friends at the Vientiane-Nong Khai border checkpoint, so I arranged for the usual few bottles of Johnny Walker Black to be delivered to them before I made a call to see if Joel's entry visa had shown up on records over the past fortnight. That proved, unfortunately, to be a negative. As is generally the case in the private eye business, nothing is simple, even though clients often assure you that it will be! Tracking down the recently un-sighted Saskatchewanian was going to entail more than a few phone calls.

Mukdahan is a small city in Thailand's far northeast, on the banks of the Mekong river. It has a sister city in Laos sitting almost opposite called Savannakhet. Border crossings here are not very common, but do happen, and I could imagine that to the uninitiated sitting in a Vietnamese café staring at a map, it would appear to be a more direct route to travel overland to Thailand.

At the time, I also had to see if a wayward Pattaya bargirl was at her home in the neighbouring province of Ubon Ratchathani. Deciding to package the two investigations together, I opted for a rental car and a couple of days driving, which in upcountry Thailand is as hazardous an undertaking as any I faced in my whole time as a PI. Inebriated motorists, crazed bus drivers high on No-Doze, families of four or five all perched precariously on small motorcycles, and itinerant buffalo that tend to charge across highways from time to time all add to the perils of road travel there in the Kingdom of Smiles.

I drove as far as Ubon Ratchatani, where the Pathumrat Hotel disco had been an interesting venue in the past, and was I looking forward to again checking out the local talent! After a short nap and a meal, I was ready to take on the night, so I slipped the disco manager a few hundred baht to secure a table in a prime location – and also to allow me to take my bottle of Jack Daniels in with me, which I trusted would attract a few of the local lovelies in my direction.

It wasn't too long before my interest was well and truly aroused: a very raunchy Thai singer bounced out and served up a fair rendition of *"Rong Dung Dung"*, which means along the lines of "sing out loudly" and is a hit made famous by Palmy, the Thai answer to Alanis Morisste. I quickly summoned a nearby waiter and poured Miss Ubon a stiff JD, which wasn't the only thing stiff in the nightclub at that point. The drink was passed up to her, lots of smiles were exchanged, and she knocked it back like a trouper. Things were looking up. I even offered a decent tip to the waiter, who only then thought to tell me the singer was married to the drummer. The frivolities sort of went downhill from there and the long drive started to take its toll. As I had an early start in the morning, I put the top back on the remaining Jack Daniels, and retired for the evening.

I therefore woke up fairly fresh in the morning, took advantage of the hotel breakfast included in the room price, and by 9 am was on the road, in search of a small village that was home to one Metta Chaikwang, former employee of Pattaya's Freelancer Bar, and now supposedly retired, awaiting a UK visa, and looking forward to a life in Luton, England.

I didn't have to venture too far off the main road to find the village, although as usual in these instances, I was very thankful for my ability to speak Thai fluently. Rather than go to her home,

I called in to the local store and stocked up on a few travel snacks. Of course, the curious Thai shop owner wanted to know what I was doing, so, as planned, I simply said I was a friend of Metta's and, as I was in the area, had called in to say hello, but she wasn't home.

"No, she won't be home until *Songkran*," I was told, which more or less confirmed what I needed to know, without alerting the family. I had been reasonably sure that it would only be the Thai New Year family reunion that would see her leave the bright-lights and comforts of Pattaya for the somewhat dull and boring life in a small Thai village.

I drove slowly past the Chaikwang family home, noting that it was one of the better ones in the village, which to the cynical Thai Private Eye man, either meant the family owned a business or had some good-looking daughters. I pulled out my camera and clicked off a few shots. The only sign of life was a plump middle-aged woman hanging out some washing, none of which would have ever graced the lithe form of a 45-kilogram bargirl.

That task completed, I continued on to Mukdahan, and by lunchtime, was seated in the Ploy Hotel restaurant, gazing out across the Mekong at neighbouring Laos. Figuring a quick afternoon chat with the local Immigration officers might go a fair way towards completing the second chore, I picked up a bottle of Johnny Walker Black and sauntered down to find their office. There were only two men present. The senior one asked in halting

English what I was after, obviously relieved when I answered him in Thai. I told him my young brother had gone missing, and I wanted to know if he had entered the Kingdom recently. I was then asked for my passport, proof that I was indeed a family member, even though I had used the Thai word "*nong*", which covers not only an actual brother or sister, but is also conveniently used to include younger relatives or even friends. The officer then went on to point out the difference between my surname and the one I had written down and was querying about. He then explained that such information could not be given to anyone who was not a direct relative.

Mmmm; that crackdown on corruption across the Kingdom might be good for Thailand's reputation worldwide, I thought, but it certainly wasn't a lot of help to the average PI. As I had found over the years, the seemingly simple approach to getting my queries answered seldom works, which is why I always try and have a Plan B ready. I picked up my bottle of Johnny, politely thanked the men for their time, and headed down to the nearby jetty. I paid a departure fee, and waited for the next ferry across the river to Savannakhet. I was sure the anti-corruption drive had not as of yet found its way into Laos! Picking up a bag of pineapple from a vendor while waiting, I learnt that the previous Immigration chief had recently been sacked – or as they politely term it, removed to an inactive post. No wonder the new man was playing things by the rules ... for now anyway.

It only took a few minutes to complete the crossing, and a 100 baht tip to a young official got me personally delivered to the local head of the Savannakhet Immigration office. My command of Lao was not great, but, along with a combination of Thai and a 1000 baht note to go with the Johnny Walker, I was soon shown the ledger of all foreigners who had exited Laos at Savannakhet in the past month. Luckily, there was only one Canadian on the list: Joel had crossed into Thailand ten days previously.

I thanked my new Laotian friend profusely, declining the offer to share some whiskey with him. I wanted to catch the next ferry back, as dusk was approaching. Safely ferried back across the river, I alighted and shortly afterwards adjourned once more to the Ploy restaurant. I opted for the *pla nin,* a very tasty type of perch, while I contemplated my next move. Or, more to the point, Joel's possible moves over the previous ten days.

Mukdahan is something of a sleepy hollow, and although there was no doubt the obligatory massage parlour and karaoke venue (or two) secreted away somewhere, it certainly is not a place known for its nightlife. I found a small Internet café and shot off a quick email to Betty and Harry, who I knew would be relived to know that Joel had safely navigated Vietnam and Laos. I also asked them if Joel had made any mention of, or had any tendencies towards, Buddhism, and if so, could they confirm ASAP.

I then headed back to the hotel, making a mental note that not too many Bangkok bargirls seem to hail from this province, and that whilst everyone I came into contact with was most friendly and polite, there was a noticeable lack of any potential movie stars or models. In fact, the last time I had ventured to Mukdahan had been on behalf of a client who was due to marry the love of his life, until my further investigation revealed that his intended was a male – and I was fairly sure that a same sex marriage was not what my client had in mind!

I took a detour, passing by the local bus and train stations to see if anyone had any recollection of Joel, but although a number of locals claimed to have seen him, or someone similar, I was aware it was more a matter of trying to be helpful rather than factual. After all, we Caucasians all look the same to them!

At most upcountry hotels, things are normally quiet mid-week, unless one of the many conferences that Thais love to organize is in progress. The Ploy Hotel was no exception, so, not surprisingly, the rather bored night manager came over to say "*Sawadee khap*", perhaps in the mistaken belief I was someone of importance, as I savoured a quiet JD and Coke. I asked him to share a drink, which proved to be a worthwhile offer, as in return for this courtesy, he told me I was welcome to pop down early in the morning and use the office computer to check my email. That was most helpful indeed, as it would save me waiting until 10 am for the Internet shops to open.

A brisk "You have mail" greeted me the following morning,

when, yet again fresh and bright, I made myself at home in the small office behind the hotel reception and logged on to the hotel computer. Betty had answered, most pleased to know her son was now in Thailand, and wondering if I was psychic: Joel had indeed mentioned in his last email that he was interested in visiting some temples and learning a little more about Buddhist beliefs.

Whether it's being psychic, having intuition, sixth sense, or more likely just a combination of those added to commonsense and experience, I regularly seemed to come up with an answer that at first appeared unlikely, but ultimately proved correct. It was a handy attribute in my field.

Seeing temples and monks everywhere, noting their calm manner, the respect the locals have for them, and indeed the overall friendly manner of most Southeast Asian people, it's not at all surprising that many travellers want to learn more about the culture and beliefs behind it all.

Psychic Thai Private Eye therefore put two and two together, added in Joel's background as far as I knew of it, and surmised that a rather studious, slight and non-sporty young man might find the call of the popular Wat Pha Nana Chat monastery in nearby Ubon Ratchatani province very enticing.

It was just under a two-hour drive to the monastery, situated in a forest reserve. The more modern, contemporary buildings, especially the main temple, stood in stark contrast to the usual ancient Khamen-influenced temples in the region I was used to visiting. Again, speaking Thai and knowing the procedure meant it was easy for me to find the new arrivals, who were busy learning meditation chants. There are certainly no ties or hold over anyone at any Thai Buddhist temple, so it was just a matter of waiting for that particular chant to be completed and then motioning to the amber-robed young Canadian who looked somewhat more gaunt than his photo, but nonetheless was easy to spot amongst the half dozen Westerners present.

Joel was more than happy to have a talk and admitted to having become so engrossed in his latest beliefs that he had forgotten to update his parents. I know it's against principle, but I would have bet Betty and Harry's retainer that the fertile forest grounds also grew a few special mushrooms or some green-leafed herb other than coriander amongst the undergrowth.

We had a pleasant chat for an hour or so. Joel wanted to know a lot about the people and the region. I took a picture of him that I said I would send to his parents, and he let me in on his latest plan. A fellow student had told him of a place in Goa where you could buy perfect wooden pipes for just a few cents. You could then sell them in the West for a few dollars, and easily subsidize your travels. Joel was going to buy a thousand and take the Saskatoon pipe market by storm. He was enjoying his time at the monastery, but told me he and his friends had been worried when this morning at dawn prayers, one of the head monks had come to the rear of the temple to sit with them. He said occasionally they had failed to take things seriously, and wondered if perhaps he was being checked up on, or if his stay at the monastery was in jeopardy. I noted an old, senior Thai monk nearby, so I went over to pay my respects, and to see if he could shed some light on Joel's standing within the community.

I returned a few moments later, and assured Joel he had no problem. Apparently the monk had been demoted and sent to sit at the back with the new arrivals. This was not because they needed checking up on, but because the particular Thai monk concerned had unfortunately had some "improper thoughts" the previous evening; hence, the demotion.

I wished Joel well in his pipe-selling venture, gave him my number just in case he did run into any difficulty while in the Kingdom, and told him I would pass on his love to his parents when I emailed them later. I would also explain to them that contact with the outside world is difficult from a Thai monastery.

It was early afternoon as I drove out of the monastery grounds; with any luck, I thought, I would be back in Bangkok by midnight. There had been the occasional Thai girl who had suggested a stint at a temple to earn merit would not do me any harm, and the odd time that I had considered such a step. However, I now had a family I wanted to be with, and besides, on trips like this, or staked out overnight watching apartment blocks, I certainly didn't lack for time to meditate.

As the Buddhist temples in Thailand are something of a

sanctuary, it has often been a strategy of nefarious politicians, about-to-be-found-out husbands, or straight-out criminals to suddenly feel the call of the temple and trust that by the time they step back into the real world, their misdeeds will be forgotten, or charges against them dropped. I had on numerous occasions had Western men inform me that their Thai girlfriends had been out of contact, because they had gone to stay at a temple. Now whilst there are indeed one or two temples for women only (a female is not allowed to touch a Thai monk, or even pass food directly to him), I have yet to see a working girl return to the Bangkok night scene with a shaven head. Still, I haven't seen the tooth fairy either, and my daughter assures me she is alive and well.

Slowly the miles were eaten up, and it was dusk as I passed my personal favourite temple and religious retreat, the ancient Khamen temple of Phanom Roong, looking much as it would have a few thousand years earlier. Not long afterwards, it was the outskirts of Saraburi, and eventually the distant twinkling lights of Bangkok could be seen.

I had another premonition that it might be some time before I was travelling that way again, and the amber robes of the monks I had seen close up during the day, I reminded myself, do not represent the sunrise, as many think, but, in fact, the sunset.

PART TWO: THE NEW ORDER

NEW TEAM, OLD PROBLEMS

"When you have a Thai girlfriend, you never lose her,
you just sometimes lose your place in the queue"
Thai Private Eye maxim

As the new management gradually took over, a number of changes became necessary.

A lot more staff, or operatives as we call them, were put on the payroll. Each case was given a number, and usually three or four operatives were assigned to each individual job, which was run by a case manager or "Control", often the Company Director, who coordinated movements from the central Bangkok office. An early case that indicates how things work resulted from an email received from Mary, a resident of the Big Apple. (New York, of course; is there any other Big Apple?) It was apparent that her "Chubby Hubby" as he soon became known, was no longer the big apple of her eye!

Mary had concerns over the frequent business trips her spouse and a business partner had been making to Asia and wondered if perhaps he was being unfaithful. As one of our agents remarked, "She may have just as well asked us if McDonalds was still selling Big Macs."

A standard questionnaire was emailed to Mary, and shortly thereafter, we had all the information required, including flight details and a picture of the big man himself. "BIG" certainly was the operative word: our quarry was bordering on morbidly obese. Six-foot-six and festooned with a number of tattoos: it was obvious that identifying this man was certainly not going to be a problem.

Mary's request was for photographic and, if possible, video evidence as proof of infidelity, for if her suspicions were confirmed, she planned to confront him and file for divorce.

As you can well imagine, in a city such as Bangkok, with over ten million people and chaotic traffic, following subjects is not always as simple as it appears in the movies. With that in mind, we always try to cover all possible angles. In this case then, three agents were allocated to handle what we called the "Chubby Hubby" case. After all, we wanted to maintain our good reputation as we are well aware of what damage any smallish company can suffer from a bad report on a website or bitter exchanges in a chatroom. We did not wish to join Chubby Hubby on Mary's list of serious disappointments.

Agent #1 was stationed in the arrival hall; his task was to

identify the subject, then follow him and get details of the taxi or mini-van he hired to take him into the city. At this stage, Agent #2, waiting in a nearby vehicle, would take over and follow the target to his hotel, which we had been informed was the Radisson, one that offered very reasonable rates for such a fine establishment. A possible reason for this is that it is some distance from the popular red-light districts. Many people making hotel bookings online don't realize the average travel time around Bangkok is 5 km per hour. We were fairly confident that Chubby Hubby would be taking another lengthy taxi ride shortly after he checked in. Agent #3 then was stationed in the Radisson Hotel lobby, slowly perusing the Bangkok *Post*.

It was not difficult for Agent #1 to spot what resembled a slow-moving hippo making its way through the throngs at the Arrivals gate some time after Flight TG 791 from New York had landed. As Mary had indicated, out target had a travelling companion, only slightly slimmer and with a shining, billiard-ball head. Spotting our pair in the local bars or clubs amongst mostly petite Thais did not seem like it was going to present any major problem.

About that time, our agent had a smug little smile on his face, content in the knowledge he had the quarry in sight, he knew his movements, and all was well in investigation land. That, however, is just about the time when things can start to turn to custard! Was this about to happen yet again? The pair of intrepid businessmen did not waddle towards the taxi queue or appear to have a welcome sign and courtesy vehicle from the Radisson on hand. Instead, they started the slow trek along the walkway signposted "Domestic"

Agent #1 hurriedly called into Control, who instructed him to follow the pair discreetly and then advised Agents #2 and #3 to stand by. Finally, the two arrivals from New York exited the walkway and headed for the Business Class check-in at Bangkok Airways, where a sign proclaimed "Koh Samui - 40 flights daily". Koh Samui is an idyllic island just off the Thai coastline, an hour's flight from Bangkok.

So much for the best-laid plans – and typical of the type of thing that can go wrong, no matter how well prepared you may be. Agent #1 notified Control, who asked him to get a couple of pictures of the pair and to also confirm the Samui flight number and see that the subjects made it on board. Agents #2 and #3 were told to stand down, and a hurried call was made to an operative we had stationed on Koh Samui. Fortunately, it was not around the time of the full moon or he may well have been plunked on the outer island of Phangnan, along with a few thousand backpackers, doing his imitation of Leonardo Di Caprio in *The Beach*.

One thing was very clear, however: this certainly was no business trip, although that had been a foregone conclusion. Mary was quickly updated as to the change in situation, and advised that expenses might add up. She was not at all pleased to learn of Chubby's change of schedule, or that additional costs would be incurred. However, she gave the go-ahead to continue the assignment. It was made very clear to her not to make mention of Koh Samui should Hubbby call her; amazing how many clients just can't help themselves at times, and totally endanger operations. More on that later!

Our Koh Samui agent got a rushed briefing. It was not quite an hour's flight to the tiny island paradise which locals have nicknamed "Little Frankfurt", such is its popularity with Germans.

Our local operative arrived at the quaint airport nestled amongst the palm trees just as the flight was taxiing to the terminal. Without bothering to dismount from his trendy Phantom Honda 200cc, he soon spotted the wayward travellers. Most travel around the island is by way of motorcycle, or little taxi vans that have been designed to carry 45-kilogram Thais. All the huffing and puffing that Chubby and his friend took to get on board meant our agent could hardly miss them!

The agent followed the taxi van at a distance, and watched as most of the passengers alighted at various hotels and along the popular Chaweng beach area. Finally, only the two heavyweights remained in the back, and the little van chugged further along the island ring road, eventually pulling into a rather isolated but exclusive resort in the next, somewhat smaller bay, appropriately known as Chaweng Noi, or little Chaweneg.

Our local agent was on good terms with almost every receptionist in the area; well, certainly the good-looking ones, so it was a simple matter to confirm that the two were booked in for a week, and that, in fact, they were in Rooms 102 and 103, poolside on the ground floor.

Sure that they were not going far for some time, he got back to Control with the details, and showing the initiative we try to install in our operatives, was able to add that Rooms 207 to 209 were opposite on a higher level, with a very nice view of the entrances to Rooms 102 and 103.

A reservation was made, and the very lucky Agent #1, having already sighted the plump pair at the airport, was told he would be able to swap his rather seedy apartment in Bangkok's Pratunam district temporarily for Room 208 at a luxury resort on Koh Samui.

Agent #1 arrived at the Koh Samui resort the following day, and was met by our local operative, who took him to the resort and supplied him with some high-definition cameras and videos.

Upmarket resort that it was, it featured dark-tinted windows, perhaps to lessen the heat, but, of course, ideal for our purposes as well. Things were all going to plan; for us, anyway!

The best method of transport around Samui is motorcycle; however, the little Honda models for rent everywhere were not suitable for Chubby and his friend, who were reduced to travelling in the taxi trucks. This, of course, made tracking them fairly simple, especially as our Samui man knew the entire island so well. With Agent #1 as the video-shooting pillion passenger, ample footage of the ample pair cavorting with local girls in bars around Chaweng and Lamai was soon obtained.

On a couple of occasions, Chubby even obliged by bringing girls back to his room for the night; although in one instance, the word "girl" had to be seriously questioned. Transvestites (or, as they are known locally, *katooeys*) abound on Samui. However, according to our agents, Chubby had most likely overlooked the larger feet, hands, and protruding Adam's apple, as he remained totally focused on a very impressive pair of silicone-filled breasts.

Chubby's new friend's prominent mammaries were, no doubt, courtesy of one of the many Bangkok clinics that specialize in cosmetic surgery. Just how much surgery the sexually reconfigured Thai male had undergone we shall never know, but certainly, on this occasion anyway, he/she was not hurriedly sent packing by a suddenly very embarrassed client!

The choice of that particular overnight companion was also something of a bonus for our cameraman. Unlike their genuine female counterparts, who even though, admittedly usually in a drunken or drug-induced haze, seem happy to dance naked around silver poles in bars, most Thai girls will revert to being shy and demure out in public or in a hotel environment. Thailand's lady-boys, however, are normally very extroverted. Extra short and/or tight-fitting is their preferred mode of dress, and, of course, they are not at all shy about showing off their silicone-enhanced assets.

All this made the footage of the loving couple in Room 103 having a poolside breakfast so much easier to obtain. That spectacle sort of resembled a whale devouring plankton, and was certainly going to go down well with Mary's lawyers, although we thought it perhaps wise for all concerned not to bring the gender of his companion into the equation at this point.

Our agents also obtained some receipts from a rubbish bin outside the Bangkok Bank's Chaweng Beach ATM machine after the target had made a withdrawal, to further confirm his whereabouts. In addition, courtesy of the resort's night manager (who had unfortunately invested his last week's wages on a below-par Arsenal that had gone down to the Spurs), they were able to get a copy of his bill that included breakfasts for two, extensive mini-bar usage, and a number of spicy Thai snacks that had been charged to his room.

All the evidence was then compiled on a DVD and couriered to Mary before the hard-working businessman returned home. She, and no doubt her lawyers too, were very happy with the result, and obviously her Chubby Hubby had a lot more to think about on his return than lithe Thai bodies and Koh Samui's nightlife and resorts.

As is often the case, it appears our "interfering" had not gone down well with the wayward hippo, as shortly afterwards, we received another email, allegedly from Mary, but strangely enough, the sentences and grammar were somewhat different in style, as was the IP address.

Supposedly, our deeply satisfied client was going on a world tour, and would be in Bangkok for a day or two. She would like to personally thank us and hand over a bonus; could we arrange to meet her?

A quick courtesy call confirmed Mary had no intentions of setting foot anywhere on the Asian continent. Control then sent a very nice reply, reminding "Mary" of our security services if she needed them, attaching the pictures of some of our Thai team whose kick-boxing prowess made Jean-Claude van Damme in his prime look about as lethal as a stunned mullet.

Suspecting that Chubby perhaps had some rather pernicious thoughts in mind for TPE (and yes, there are some very vindictive people out there, again something we will come to shortly), Control couldn't help but add a little "P.S." to the email. It read, "It was indeed sad to discover your husband's sexual preferences have changed. I suppose a reason for his booking into such a secluded resort was this penchant he has developed for young males and transvestites."

For some reason, we never got a reply to this message or heard from the sender again.

NEVER A DULL MOMENT

*"Never attribute to malice
that which can be explained by mere stupidity."*
Anonymous

I mentioned that things don't always go to plan in the world of investigations, and also that vindictiveness is something that perhaps is more often on some clients' minds than they let on.

With regard to things going awry, one very vivid episode still stands out in my memory.

I had been investigating a traditional Thai massage worker. As it happened, she hailed from Buriram province in the northeast, and consequently, in addition to Thai, she also spoke Khamen, a Cambodian dialect. From my earlier times managing a hotel in neighbouring Surin, I was one of the few Westerners who had some knowledge of that language.

I had initially struggled to get much information out of the lady concerned and had learnt she was a very well-trained and thorough masseuse, and in two visits as a client, I had found she was 100% straight in the art of performing traditional Thai massage only. I also had walked out with muscles aching in places I didn't even know I had muscles!

To get a little closer to her, to try and unlock any secrets she may have had about her love life, and, in particular, to find out how enamoured she was of my client, I had reverted to speaking with her in Khamen. The Thai class system being what it is, Bangkokians tend to look down on those from upcountry who also speak Lao, as many people from the Northeast or I-sarn region do, and to speak Khamen seems to put one even lower down the Thai social ladder.

I had soon learnt, however, that being able to speak that dialect brought me much closer to the people of Surin, Buriram and Si-saket, many of whom had Cambodian heritage, and, quite coincidentally, were to be found working in the local night trade.

This girl, apart from possessing that somewhat unique Thai-Cambodian brand of beauty, was likewise much more friendly and forthcoming when she found I knew her native language. I was then able to find that, contrary to my client's beliefs, she was not deeply in love with him, but simply saw him as a friend or father figure.

The client was not really happy, or, I suspect, didn't totally believe me when I reported this back to him. Valentine's Day was approaching, and although he could not be there on the day itself, he had planned a surprise visit a day or two later. He then asked me to purchase a gold bracelet and have it secretly delivered to the lady on February 14th. It was obviously a rather busy day for a private eye, and although I could have asked one of my assistants to drop it off, there were many girls working at that particular massage centre, so I wanted to make sure it was delivered to the right one.

I guess my mistake was in not using one of my regular motorcycle taxi boys, but it was hot, and I was en route to another job, so I had just hailed an air-con taxi from outside the gold shop. I explained to the driver that we needed to stop briefly outside the massage centre, and that I would give him a 200 baht bonus for quickly going in and delivering the package to Miss Metta from Buriram. All seemed to be fine: I sat back in the taxi watching to see that the driver didn't palm the bracelet or pull some such trick. I saw him approaching at the counter, then handing the package over as planned to the right girl. In less than a minute, he came back out, full of smiles, got into the cab, but ignored my cries of "*Bai, bai*" (the Thai word for "go").

You can probably guess what happened next. Miss Metta, looking resplendent in special Valentine's Day attire, came rushing out, desperate to thank her new-found beau. I'm sure if I had asked the driver to head straight to the nearest short-time hotel, it would have been no problem and a very exciting time would have been had by both of us. Of course, that would not have impressed my client, so I had to turn down her advances, and admit that my visits, and the gift, had been on behalf of someone rather more keen to marry her than I was.

She, of course, was not overjoyed that perhaps I didn't really like her – or, more to the point, that I had been somewhat devious, and certainly was not at all impressed that her prospective beau would stoop to such activity. When the client called in a few days later to find out how things had gone, he himself was not at all complimentary, and thought that I had about as much skill as an investigator as Inspector Clouseau on psychotropic drugs!

A more recent case that went awry happened when we were contacted by Sybil, an elderly, well-spoken British lady who asked us to conduct surveillance on her 65-year-old husband.

Having been married almost 40 years, she thought she knew his habits rather well. However, he had lately taken to gallivanting around the globe with a particularly well-endowed Russian lady. The wife had gained access to his email, so she had been keeping track of his exploits as he updated friends on his escapades. Sybil assured us (though such assurances do not mean a lot to a cynical PI) that she was not at all interested in his sexual conquests, but simply wanted to put a stop to the spending spree that was fast diminishing their grandchildren's education fund.

That the "Ageing Lothario" (as we named him) would bother to bring the busty Muscovite to Bangkok seemed to us a little like taking coal to Newcastle, but Sybil was the client, she was the one paying, and she assured us she had all the information regarding his schedule.

Shortly afterwards, along with a retainer, we received details of his flight from Tokyo to Bangkok, their hotel booking, pictures of them both, and a description of his luggage. A rather straightforward case, it seemed, of following them to their pre-booked hotel and taking a few pictures along the way. What could be easier?

As is our usual mode of operation, a three-man team was assigned. One was stationed at the Arrivals hall, another in a car nearby, and the third booked into his hotel, positioned in the lobby, reading. Flight AA5832 from Tokyo landed on time around 9 pm, but an hour later it seemed all passengers had disembarked, with no sign of anyone resembling our quarry.

Had our agent missed him? Had he been waylaid by Immigration? Had a heart attack? Control told the agents to stay put and to check out the later flight from Tokyo, due in around midnight. This proved to be rather astute advice, as the British gentleman was, indeed, spotted coming through Arrivals with the exodus from that later flight.

There was, however, no sign of any Russian female companion, well-built or otherwise. Also notable was the apparent lack of baggage for a world traveller; our target had just one small piece of hand luggage. Had his luggage been forwarded directly to the hotel? Perhaps there had been a mix-up and it was on the earlier flight. Or maybe someone else, such as the mysterious Russian lady, had his luggage.

All a little strange really for a "straightforward" case. However, for the moment it was a matter of just passing on the details of the taxi he hailed to Agent #2, who dutifully followed him to his city hotel. At that stage, the case was handed over to Agent #3, who had been waiting patiently in the hotel lounge. He confirmed that Sybil's wayward husband had checked in and retired to his room. Agent #1 had remained at the airport, just to see if Miss Moscow did in fact appear, and was rewarded some 20 minutes later with seeing an indeed well-endowed blonde. Said blonde was doing a good imitation of a has-been movie star, pushing a trolley laden down with designer blue luggage along with Mr Lothario's distinctive brown suitcase.

By this time, of course, our own vehicle was back in the city, so our agent hailed an airport taxi and tried to follow the buxom blonde. This only got him about as far as the first freeway tollbooth, where he lost her in a maze of taxis. No problem: our agent at the hotel was alerted to await her pending arrival. And so he waited. And waited. By 3 am, it was obvious that she was a no-show, and thoughts that this wasn't quite going according to script really started to multiply.

The agent at the hotel was told to get a few hours sleep, but to be down in the dining hall when it opened for breakfast at 7 am. Then, once Lothario appeared, some back-up would be sent to help track his movements for the day.

First thing our agent did when he went downstairs in the morning was the standard scrutinizing of room keys behind the front desk. Our quarry's room key was in plain view!

Checking with hotel staff confirmed that we had the right room number, but a number of calls to the room yielded no answer. Perhaps he had gone for an early morning walk, so we remained at the hotel until midday, as the expense account tally for cups of coffee mounted rapidly!

Finally, we realized we had been given the slip, so Control had the disappointing task of contacting Sybil with the news.

"Oh," said Sybil, "I thought he may be on his guard, as I did have a local firm follow him to the same hotel about six months ago, so I immediately got on a plane, flew to Bangkok, and confronted him in the room."

Suffice it to say we were not all that pleased or impressed. Often, in fact, the cause of cases going awry is because they are compromised by the client. Like Sybil, they neglect to give you the full background, or else at some stage in the job, they can't help but let the subject know some snippet of covert information that has been gathered. Of course, there is also then the danger of having our operatives being confronted by very irate husbands, girlfriends, or – worse – girlfriends' husbands! Revenge and vindictiveness are traits that do surface often amongst a number of our clients and targets.

For instance, we recently handled a straightforward case for an Australian woman. Yes, her husband was having an affair with a local bargirl. Love had been pledged, marriage plans formed, and, of course, monies promised. Unbeknown to him, however, he was not the only sponsor of this particular lovely, but that is nothing unusual.

The average wage in Thailand probably falls into the US$200-300 per month range. When a working girl is used to earning five or even ten times that average monthly wage by way of bar fines, tips, payment for extracurricular activities, not to mention monthly retainers from various sponsors, she won't always settle for a basic monthly payment whilst she awaits a visa or attends school. After experiencing the bright city lights and easy money, going back home and planting rice just does not have the same allure. Moreover, her family by then has most likely become accustomed to monthly cash handouts and they don't want those flows to cease either. However, I digress.

Not completely happy just with the evidence, or the fact that her husband was himself being two-timed, the women wanted us to "beat the girl up a bit". When we advised her that that was not something we could be part of, she then wanted us to "cut her hair off" so she couldn't work in the bar scene for a while. That was the end of our discussion. We didn't even bother to inform her that some very fine wigs are made in Thailand.

This was not the only time we were asked to perform some

activity that went far beyond what we were willing to do. Another such case involved a sixty-year-old Canadian man who contacted us. We immediately sympathized with this gentleman's plight: his legal and, yes, somewhat younger Thai wife had emptied their Thai bank account and also sold, or at least transferred, the new home he had built to her parents. This could be done simply, as land must, under Thai law, be in the wife's, or some other Thai national's name.

All this happened while he was back in Edmonton, on a final trip to tie up all the loose ends, sell his house and car, put the dog to sleep, and say farewell to friends and family. Then it was a return to Thailand and his loving young wife, to complete the retirement move he had been planning and saving for over the past few years. On his return, and finding out just what had happened, he contacted the local police. Later, with the help of a Thai lawyer, he did get his now ex-wife into court. In true Thai fashion, she was found guilty only of a minor offence relating to the transfer of the house.

She was ordered to pay him half the value of the house and half the amount in the joint bank accounts they had. This was to be completed within ten years. However, by this time the money had either been spent or perhaps was in some Thai boyfriend's account, and the house was in her parent's name. This had all happened three years before we were contacted, and in that whole time, he had not received a single baht from her in compensation.

By now 63 years old, he didn't feel like waiting around for another seven years just to see if any of his hard-earned retirement money would be getting refunded. We had our own lawyers go over all the legal documents and court findings, to no avail. The end result: he was screwed.

He obviously, and with good cause, had brooded over this for some time. He advised us that he wanted our lawyers to be prepared to seize her assets immediately when she, his ex-wife, inherited the property from her parents. We mentioned the small matter that both parents had to be dead for this to happen. "So arrange it then," was his reply.

Even though we felt for him, we could no longer be involved, other then to simply warn him against doing anything rash or stupid. We did mention that we would monitor the health of his ex-wife's parents, as in our position we can't be even remotely involved with planned "accidents".

Certainly, hit men are available throughout many parts of Asia. Thailand is no exception. In my earlier days, through corrupt Thai associates as well as my knowledge of Cambodia and the Khamen language, I certainly knew where to find them. Cambodian army or former Khmer Rouge operatives would regularly cross the border on such missions, while for a more reliable hit, the eastern seaboard city of Chonburi had the dubious distinction of being something of a hitman's haven, a small hotel in nearby Baeng Saen being a well-known meeting point.

Today, however, Thai laws and regulations are much tighter, and apart from in the movies, or the rare, usually monetarily motivated hit, drive-by assassinations are no longer common.

One overly vindictive South African was very keen for us to perform a "hit" for him. Now usually we do not even meet with prospective clients, one reason being we ourselves may well be on the wrong end of some vindictiveness. This Yarpie, however, was very keen to meet and discuss his problem and more than happy to pay well. A time and place was arranged after some preliminary background checks had confirmed that he was indeed a successful businessman in his home country and that he had a very expensive condo in Soi Thonglor.

Two of our security men were stationed nearby when we went to meet up. From his appearance, however, this fellow was probably more in need of security than was our man. With designer clothes, a Rolex (and presumably not a cheap Chatujak Market fake either), a large diamond ring and an obnoxious-looking gold chain round his neck clasping a diamond-studded medallion, he looked like some high-class pimp, but, hey, whatever turns you on. As a rule, however, openly flaunting wealth in countries like Thailand is not very smart.

He explained the position (well, his version of it anyway) to us in this way: He had been due to head to the airport, as he had to spend a few weeks checking up on his business commitments back in Cape Town before again returning to relax in Bangkok. He had left his Thai girlfriend (his choice of words, although perhaps paid-for-companion or, as Bernard Trink would say, "demimondaine" was a more accurate description) in the apartment while he went down to the office, paid some bills and locked up his car.

Apparently, when he went back up to his condo to pick up his bags, the girl, who in standard Thai girlfriend fashion was supposed to have accompanied him to the airport, was gone. The demimondaine was not all that was missing. Also gone, so he said, was about US$2,000 in cash, US$3,000 in gold and jewellery, plus 200,000 Thai baht that he was about to put into the condo safe. As he had to be at the airport, he said that he didn't have time to go to the police, so he hailed a taxi and thought he would sort things out when he returned a few weeks later.

We are well aware that a client's version of events may often differ from the actual facts. However, although there were a number of question marks surrounding his narrative, as usual, we could only question them and move on. Just why you would have that much cash on hand, and in plain view, is itself questionable. However, he said he often left large sums of money around, and she never took any notice. He said he had even tested her at times, leaving an exact amount of cash on a bedside cabinet and his lady friend had never touched anything.

"She only had to ask if she needed anything," he said. "I gave her plenty of spending money and even built a house for her family."

It was pointed out to him that now that she had shown her true colours, he was fortunate not to have married the girl: she may well have ended up with the condo and 50% of his wealth! This, however, was not what he wanted to hear. He had his own version of he truth: "She only took the money because her Thai boyfriend made her." He then added, "I want him terminated." Thai boyfriend, love triangles, revenge, "termination" – this was all getting a little sticky suddenly. We informed him that we certainly would not be involved in any acts of revenge he may have been contemplating and that it seemed like a straightforward case for the local police.

We then tried to justify our time and meeting by explaining some of the ways and wherefores of Thai life, and said that while it was unfortunate, the best one could do was simply put it down to life's experiences and move on. Certainly, being in Bangkok and throwing money around as he did, attracting a new girlfriend wouldn't be any problem.

He was, however, adamant on the revenge theme. "I heard it's possible to buy a hit on someone for a few thousand dollars here," he said. His emotional stability was now being seriously called into question. When told this was certainly something we would not be in any way involved with, he became quite irate, and stormed off a rather distressed and angry man.

We assumed that was the last we would see of the Cape Town crusader, but alas, not so. Two weeks later, he again got into contact with us. This time he wanted us to find an Austrian man so we could "get his money back". Just what money was this, we asked.

He then told us how he had been put in touch with this man by a person he had met in a bar in Pattaya. He had been assured the guy could help him with his revenge problem. However, the due date of the hit had come and gone, and apparently the Thai boyfriend was still alive and well. In fact, he was even sporting a brand new motorbike. The only "hit" to speak of had been for another US$3,000 on the South African's pocket! He was now offering to pay us even more money to track down the guy he had "donated" this latest payment to.

The Cape Town kid was something of a loose canon, and certainly one we didn't want to be involved with. Just where or who he is with now I have no idea, but he had the right type of attitude to get himself into some very serious trouble in a land he had little knowledge of or respect for. It never ceases to amaze me how people who may be very astute in the business or "real" world issues somehow seem to lose the plot when in Thailand – especially when confronted with nubile Thai lasses dancing around silver poles!

As I often end up saying to male clients, when you arrive in Bangkok, you usually have a lot of money and are looking for a cute Thai girl who has some experience. By the time you leave, she has the money and you have had the experience.

Of course, as we saw above, vindictiveness is not just a characteristic of the male of the species. We once received an email from a woman about a particular person who, according to her, was a danger to young girls.

At Thai Private Eye, we obviously work closely with both local and international agencies when it seems required. More than once we have uncovered signs of paedophilia and immediately notified the relevant authorities. Of course, exactly what your definition of "young" is can differ, and when questioned, the client said the young ladies involved might have been in the 18 to 20-year-old bracket.

Obviously, both our client and the intended quarry were much older. We didn't bother to inform her that many street-smart Thai girls of that age have already acquired knowledge and experience of someone at least ten years older in the Western world. But we did carry out a little routine background check before we got involved in the case.

Our female client had made bookings for the man, who was scheduled to attend a Bangkok seminar. Obviously, she knew of, or had researched, something of the city's nightlife. She had provided us with his entire travel itinerary, down to the last detail, and we had assumed she was the worried wife. Getting what background we can on a client is important, as we wouldn't be the first agency ever to be set up. Indeed, on a number of occasions, we have uncovered efforts to do just that, set us up or in some way make us the "fall guys".

Fortunately, her real name showed on her private email account which she had used to contact us. A simple check on the company website showed that the CEO of the company was in fact the target – and that the lady who contacted us was his personal secretary! Putting two and two together, we challenged her motives. She admitted that she hated the thought of her boss coming to Bangkok and running around loose in such a "den of iniquity", as she termed it. Whether he had previously spurned her advances, or perhaps she just had a wish to take over his position, we did not know. But in any case, we told her quite firmly that we were not very taken with her attitude, and certainly would not take the case either.

THE THAIS THAT BIND

"Even a blind cat can stumble over a dead mouse sometimes."
Chinese proverb

A further advancement for the company these days is that we do employ quite a few fully trained and qualified Thai operatives. This makes the way easier for surveillance on subjects in suburbia, or in small upcountry villages where, in the past, I often carried out investigations myself and felt at times that I stood out like a miniskirt in a monastery.

One particular case we handled shows how important it can be to have multiple operatives. A successful Pattaya businessman, a Thai national, contacted us. He had heard good reports about our firm, he said. Plus, he was aware that some of the less scrupulous amongst our local competition did not always put their clients' best interests first!

A friend had spotted his wife with her former boyfriend, and mentioned it to him, so he had queried her about it. His wife's answer was that she was being stalked by her ex. The husband was not totally sure, so our brief was to confirm if his wife was indeed being stalked, in which case we could gather evidence for him to provide to the police. Or, if his suspicions had some ground to them, we could find if the two were continuing their former affair. Betting man that I am, I was making the latter a fairly warm favourite for the truth!

Considering all the variables one faces tailing people, along with the fact that the client was happy to pay good money to get the case settled quickly, we opted to use two rental cars, one just as a back-up, and also to have a motorcycle on standby. Thai number plates have the region of registration on them as well as the number, so to remain as inconspicuous as possible, we always rent locally.

Four of our Thai agents were on hand, one female. The controlling agent went along on the job as well, and doubled up as the video cameraman. We, of course, knew the day's proposed plans for our client's wife – well, at least as far as taking their children to and from school as well as the route she would take on that particular chore. Why, therefore, so much manpower for what seemed a simple observation job? Because you can never discount the pervasive power of Murphy's Law!

The Staff assignments were set out in the following way: Car #1 and driver: Keep eyes on the subject's car at all times, even when it is parked.

Spotter: This was the lady of the team, seated in the back behind the passenger seat, so she remained out of view of the subject, just in case we happened to get too close. Also, she would be able to quickly get out of the vehicle and onto the pavement if, for any reason, foot pursuit were required.

Video cameraman/Control: In the back of the car and available as back-up foot pursuit.

Motorcyclist: A further back-up, just in case there was too much traffic and we lost the subject, or if we needed to transport the spotter somewhere in a hurry.

Car #2 and driver: Kept in the vicinity in case our Car #1 was recognized.

Our team was all in place when the client called in at 7:30 am on a typical hot and sunny Pattaya morning to inform us his wife had just left the house with the children. We knew the route she took to the school, and in any event, our interest was primarily in what she did after the children were dropped off. As is our procedure when possible, we had surveyed the area previously and determined that the best place to watch the school was in a small *soi* opposite the main gate that was actually the entranceway to a large housing estate. We knew the estate security guard might question us if we were there too long, but that was unlikely, and we did have our motorcyclist plus back-up car handy if we were asked to move. All was in readiness then.

Shortly after 8 am, the team saw the children dropped off and that the driver was ready to move. The subject, however, make a quick U-turn and drove straight into the small side street we were parked in. The whole operation seemed compromised within two minutes! She, the subject, parked opposite us, got out and walked straight in front of our car. Our driver gazed at the gear lever, the spotter ducked down with her head on the lap of the cameraman, who at that point probably wished that the new, young and good-looking girl had been brought along instead of the somewhat older, chubbier one. At times like this, you always wonder just how effective those tinted windows we try to have our vehicles fitted with actually are.

Tension, followed by a sort of controlled panic, hit our team. What had gone wrong to be "made" that early in the investigation was the question they were all thinking, but didn't dare ask. Finally, daring a glance in the rear-view mirror, the driver was greeted with a startling sight.

Our client's wife was getting into another car, parked just a few metres behind his. The car certainly hadn't been there a few moments earlier – so using great powers of deduction, our driver surmised that the vehicle must have come from within the housing estate.

Slowly, the team's heart rates returned to somewhere near normal, training kicked in, a cross-check of case notes with the vehicle seen in the rear-view mirror, in which the subject was now seated, confirmed it was in fact the vehicle owned by her former boyfriend, the alleged "stalker". We had been given details of his vehicle's colour and make, but not the registration plate number, which, had we had it, would have given us his address. Far than being compromised, within half an hour we had confirmed that the woman was indeed meeting voluntarily with her ex. Sometimes things do just fall into place!

Being suddenly so close to a subject can be a little troubling, but it does, of course, make for good video footage, and the static covert camera unit placed in the rear window certainly did its job well. Soon thereafter, the woman went back to her car, made another U-turn, and then followed the alleged stalker out to the main road, tailing the rapidly disappearing boyfriend's vehicle.

Having a back-up car proved a wise precaution, as it was able to take over our careful pursuit of the woman. After all, she had clearly seen the original car and, possibly, the driver as well. With spotter and cameraman transferred to car #2, they set off to see what further eventuated.

The original driver was dispatched to the rental car company to swap vehicles, and return to the area. Like many of our drivers, Agent #2 doubled as a taxi driver when not working for us, so catching up and settling into a standard pursuit pattern was not too much of a problem. That is, until the subjects suddenly both took a right turn at an amber light and headed up a side road. Even our back-up motorcyclist missed that manoeuvre, so for all our tight planning, it seemed we had lost them.

Just as our team cursed its bad luck, the two vehicles re-appeared. They had obviously taken a wrong turn, and were now heading back in the direction they had started out from. A bit confusing, but it was another lucky break – which in our business, you need to make the most of.

Without being asked, our driver showed off some deft Bangkok taxi driver skills: a screech of tires, a cloud of blue smoke, and we were back on the chase. So much for trying to remain covert! It took a kilometre or two, but before long, the targets were back in view. No sooner had that happened, than both the vehicles we were tracking made yet another U-turn. It seemed they were deliberately trying to shake off any would-be tails! Control thought perhaps it was time to call the day's surveillance off, when wife and "stalker" both pulled into a petrol station almost opposite our car. Apparently, lack of petrol (and not abundance of caution) was the reason for the latest turn in their erratic route.

Our spotter lady scurried over to use the petrol station's toilets and got some good pictures of the pair on her mobile phone, then hurried back as the woman left her vehicle and climbed into the boyfriend's car. They then drove right past our team, back towards the school. Control sent the motorcyclist to track them, then joined up with the driver and spotter as they went into the petrol station for a coffee and to see how the photographic evidence was looking.

Things really started to make sense when we saw an attendant begin washing the woman's car. Control took his coffee back to the vehicle and called up the client, while our driver and spotter did as any Thais do when they have a chance: they went and found a food vendor. The client, somewhat subdued upon hearing that stalking was out of the equation, assured us his wife had no reason to believe she was being followed, then agreed that the motorcyclist surveillance and a watch on the car at the garage continue until his wife's return. The motorcyclist was called, and reported that the pair had stopped at a nearby shopping mall and were themselves having a coffee and what appeared to be a rather unhappy discussion. He added that he had then ducked out for a toilet break, and when he came back, the couple had gone. Perhaps not the ideal work ethic; however, this being Thailand, there was little Control could do other than to say "*Mai pen rai*". (*Mai pen rai* is a frequently used Thai phrase that translates as "never mind" or "don't worry about it". This is the Thai attitude to many problems, which foreigners often have to struggle to adapt to.)

Control had just finished speaking to the motorcyclist when a car pulled into the parking space beside him. It was the boyfriend! This was one of those times you start to wonder why you are in the investigative profession: the hairs stand up on the back of your neck and the minutes tick by very slowly. Panicky thoughts rush through your mind: is he waiting for some Thai heavies to arrive?

Will he get out in a minute, come over and start hammering on the car door? Where is the woman?

Control kept still and, he hoped (courtesy of the tinted windows), out of sight. He was slightly consoled knowing that two staff members were nearby; supposedly. Were they intent on their food, were they being cool, or had they perhaps inadvertently tipped the guy off? You start to look around for a weapon and wonder why you don't carry a flick knife or pepper spray. About this time, whether it was just nerves or that last coffee, our prime man really needed a toilet break himself. But just as he was contemplating the idea of slipping out the other side door, a car pulled into that spot, driven by the women. Out of his view, she had collected her vehicle from the car wash. The boss man, our Control agent, was now well and truly hemmed in. He crouched down in the rear seat, his bladder close to bursting, the car's air-con off and windows up, sweat dripping off him at a far heavier rate than it would at any of the city's better known sauna establishments.

However, surprisingly to him, both suspects remained oblivious to his presence. He actually could not have been in a better position now, as far as gaining evidence was concerned. The woman had walked over and was seated in the boyfriend's car. Peering cautiously through the tinted window, Control saw them in a deep and, at times, heated discussion. The camera's zoom showed her deep in thought while the guy was doing the ranting and raving, even banging the steering wheel with his fist. It did, of course, make for some great footage! Finally, she got out of the vehicle, and her ex – no, better make that "still" – boyfriend, quickly reversed out, driving off in what could only be called a huff. The women slowly ambled back to her vehicle and also drove away.

Control was at that point far more concerned with getting to the toilet than bothering to pursue them further. Besides, what had originally been estimated as a two- or three-day job had by good luck rather than good management been completed in just a few hours. A text message on Control's phone indicated that the number plate of the boyfriend's vehicle had been confirmed, along with his home address, which was, indeed, in the estate opposite the school.

The client was updated with the news. Happy with the progress, if not the result, he was going to confront the pair just as soon as he had contacted his bank and blocked his wife's access to further cash. He believed he had probably financed the old boyfriend's car and even the house, as it was.   He was asked if he wanted some back-up or moral support, but thankfully declined; he said he had a very intimidating driver of his own. We don't like to get involved in Thai domestic disputes if we can avoid them, so we just saw him at the office the next day when he picked up a detailed DVD.

He told us that at least for now, and for the child's sake,

he and his missus would remain together. He was, of course, depressed to learn of the outcome; who wouldn't be? It was now apparent his wife had been milking him for years and supporting her "former" boyfriend with some of the flow. It had only been a chance sighting of them by that friend that had resulted in him contacting us.

He was also able to shed some light on the pair's demeanour the previous day. His wife, he told us, had been on the phone to him, reminding him of the 300,000 baht he had agreed to give her to open a cosmetics business. He had then told her he had changed his mind, and they could discuss it later. Obviously, he had contacted us just in time, as no doubt much of the money was earmarked for the boyfriend, to prop up his own faltering company.

It's not often that things all fall into place so simply, but it certainly makes for a refreshing change when they do, as in this case. Of course, the case control agent, who probably aged a year or two within minutes and lost a number of kilos during the morning's activities, may not totally agree with our assessment of how simply things worked out in this case

ART FOR ART'S FAKE

*"Our admiration of the antique is not admiration
of the old, but of the natural."*
Ralph Waldo Emerson

The majority of tourists who arrive in Bangkok and want
some nearby sea and sand take the hour or two drive north
to Pattaya. Thai locals in need of the same environment usually
head a similar distance south, to Hua Hin or Cha Am. I have
learnt to never underestimate the value of local knowledge, and
in this respect came to make Cha Am my favourite convenient
getaway from the smog of Bangkok. I often took my family down
to Cha Am for a few days, where food and accommodation were
about half the cost of the same in Pattaya, and the water twice as
clean!

You also tend to meet a somewhat better standard of beach-
walker. Not that I'm knocking the more dubious beachside
inhabitants of Pattaya, or the place itself. Far from it; in fact,

we get a lot of business from that resort. However, it was always nice to travel south, especially if you could manage it mid-week. Weekends saw a huge influx as many affluent Thais from Bangkok headed down to their holiday apartments at the two seaside resorts. Even the Thai royal family has for many years maintained a holiday home in Hua Hin.

Also there in Hua Hin was Rob, an Aussie who apparently was living something like a king himself. He had, it seemed, been able to organize what I'm sure many men would consider the ideal lifestyle. Formerly a struggling small stallholder at Melbourne's famed Queen Victoria Market, a trip to Thailand some years previously had alerted him to some of the Kingdom's many elegant objects, and we are not talking demimondaines here !

Rob had upgraded his business to higher quality Asian artefacts and business had boomed. He now had three Melbourne outlets, and was about to open another in Sydney. His usual itinerary was two weeks in Melbourne organizing his shops, staff, and stock, followed by two weeks travelling around Thailand, stocking up on exquisite handicrafts, and apparently accompanied by an equally exquisite secretary named Ying, who doubled as his girlfriend.

Rob had obviously done his homework and had things well worked out. We weren't sure we would buy a used car off him, but we had to admire the way he had structured his lifestyle.

The lovely Ying had a good background, was a graduate of

Chiang Mai University, and had the classic high cheekbone and pale skin of the girls from that area. In many cases, this came , along with family wealth, from a distant relationship to affluent Chinese who in generations past had decided to forsake various people's revolutions and flee south with their assets. Family wealth was also frequently associated with such a pedigree.

Chiang Mai is seen as perhaps the art and cultural centre of Thailand, so having a local to negotiate on his behalf at the many factories on the city's outskirts that produced high-class jewellery, Buddhist amulets, teak furniture and related treasures was a wise move, quite apart from the fact that Ying was a perfect model for showing off his latest purchases in the company brochures.

From Chiang Mai, the couple would head Rob's trendy Jeep across country to the eastern province of Surin and a small village known as Ban Khwao Sinarin, where the locals had for hundreds of years carried on a Cambodian art of crafting fine silverware. More merchandise would be brought from Bangkok's Chatujak market, and they would then return to what was basically their home, a condo Rob had brought in Hua Hin. Two weeks would be spent itemizing stock, finalizing shipping and relaxing, and so the cycle continued. So what then was his problem?

With the setting up of his new Sydney outlet, Rob was going to be back in the land of koalas and kangaroos for perhaps a month this time. Considering that Ying was a very attractive and bright 25-year-old with her own car and money in the bank who also, according to Rob, was not at all averse to sex, drugs and rock&roll, he did have some anxieties – not so much about Ying's loyalty, you understand, but about how young local men might well try and distract her.

He told us it had been made clear to Ying that any association with past boyfriends, of which there had no doubt been a few, or any hint of new ones, would instantly spell the end of their association and the obviously easy-going and well-paid lifestyle to which she had quickly become accustomed. Knowing (so he thought) all the answers, Rob had also installed a landline to the condo so that he could call at anytime and confirm that she was, indeed, at their home. Nonetheless, he decided that during his upcoming extended sojourn, it would be a good time to have Ying's activities monitored, especially as he was considering making their arrangement somewhat more permanent.

He had been unsure as to her daily routine when he was away, apart from confirming that like the majority of Thai girls who didn't have a day job, she was unlikely to be seen much before mid-day! Accordingly, our team's first step was to set up covert surveillance from a vehicle parked outside the condo. Hua Hin being relatively quiet, especially during the week, it was easy to get a parking spot almost directly opposite, and the team let the video cameras run for twelve hours from 10 am until 10 pm. Admittedly, after sunset, the quality of the video was not that great, but still good enough to see who came and went. The recording was retrieved every four hours, and the vehicles rotated at the same time. The recording was then taken to our nearby base, where the rather time-consuming task of editing would begin. Sightings of Ying were then burned onto a separate DVD that we would forward to Rob in due course.

A rather boring assignment, but boring is, surprisingly, the norm for our type of work. Coverage was to last for seven days, during which time we saw the subject come and go and managed to get a good idea of her daily routine. However, as far as we were aware, she had always been on her own. The only question mark: under the current agreement, surveillance ceased at 10 pm, and on a few occasions she had not returned by then. One other significant point was that we had not yet been inside the condo, although it did appear all was fine there as well.

Rob was kept informed; one could almost note a touch of smugness as we confirmed Ying's apparent solitary existence. We then suggested, as a final check, that we rent an apartment inside the same building for a few days. As it was midweek, it was most likely there would be vacant apartments, usually rented out by owners who used the accommodations only occasionally, on weekends or holidays. Enquiries confirmed this to be so, and thus, with Rob's go-ahead, an apartment (which, the receptionist sadly informed us, lacked a sea-view) was rented for three days. Ideally for our agents, its balcony overlooked the street and condo entrance, and even better, we were able to get one on the same floor as his apartment, the current abode of an apparently lonely Miss Ying.

The old and normally reliable method of detection was the first step undertaken by our now on-site agents: the simple shoe inspection. Amazing how many two-timing Thais have been caught out simply by their adherence to established rules of good behaviour. Thai etiquette decrees that one always leaves one's shoes outside a house, apartment or temple. Outside Rob's apartment were just two pairs of women's footwear, which inspection of the daily videos confirmed had both graced Ying's dainty feet. Likewise, a check of the portable clothesline on the balcony showed no sign of anything other than female attire. It was then onto the more modern surveillance techniques in which Thai Private Eye is amongst the region's leaders these days (fortunately for Rob).

An optical-fibre Flexi-Snake cam that just slides under the door was set up, confirming the big advantage of being able to rent an apartment on the same floor. These devices do have their limitations, but are quite effective in well-lit hallways with plenty of natural light during the day. In Thailand, most apartment hallways are well lit at night for security purposes, so that also helped our operation. Not to cast any aspersions on the Thai construction industry, but the majority of Thai apartments also seem to have a noticeable gap between door and floor, although our esteemed company director believes it's just to let cockroaches come and go as they please. Nonetheless, it also proves very convenient for employing this type of camera.

The case control agent was doing the first spell in the apartment, as this required discreetly setting up the snake cam, which was placed in a sock in a specially adapted open-toed sandal outside the door. Fortunately, it was very quiet in the early afternoon, and with no one about, our man could easily check that all the angles were correct, the cables secured and fed back to the room's TV. He had barely closed the door, hooked up the DVR, got himself a cold drink and settled down to watch the main afternoon feature, "Thai Hallway", when a young man appeared on the TV screen, apparently coming out of Ying's door! Our agent had to double-check the doorway: had the man indeed exited from the targeted apartment? The confirmation he needed came a moment later when Miss Ying herself exited the very same door. A frantic call to the agents outside, who in typical Thai fashion had wandered off to find some food, soon had them back in action.

The man had disappeared, but Ying had only just stepped out onto the street, so they followed her down the road to the town's main supermarket. Being caught a little off guard, they did not have the usual covert, body-worn video cams fitted, but the high-end mobile telephone camera/videos they are issued provided a very good back-up. They managed to get stills from different angles of Ying and her friend walking around shopping, like a regular married couple, and ultimately both placing articles in the same shopping trolley.

Amazingly, once inside the store, the pair dropped their guard. Outside, however, they kept up the pretence of not knowing each other. Well, they tried to, but once we knew of the connection, it then became obvious that they were together. Thais don't normally show affection in public anyway, but from their nods and glances, walking apart but waiting for each other at crossings, there was no doubt they knew each other, and each other's habits, very well.

Meanwhile, Control was running a quick scan of the previous week's footage. Sure enough, there he was, the same guy walking just five or ten metres in front of her almost every time. Continued surveillance, and a thorough study of the tapes, would no doubt have brought the man to our attention eventually. However, once it was known who to concentrate on, it became so bloody obvious. Life certainly has become tougher for secret Thai boyfriends over the past few years!

An agent notified Control that the shopping trip was almost over and they were both at the checkout counter. He then made sure that the snake cam was fine-tuned and the footage being recorded. He also set up a Sony video camera on a tripod on the balcony to film their return. The Thai boyfriend appeared around the corner shortly thereafter, and Ying followed a little later. The beau entered the building first and headed upstairs to where the two apartments were. Sitting in his apartment, viewing the suddenly far more entertaining version of "Thai Hallway", Control saw our new target peep his head around the corner from the top of the stairwell and wait at the top of the stairs. A few moments later, he turned round and gave Ying the all-clear as she also made her way up the stairs. The crafty boyfriend opened the door and, without taking his shoes off, scraped them several times on the doormat and slipped in. Ying, being the clean, polite Thai girl that she was, took her shoes off and left them outside.

Rob was duly called and notified of the new findings. We asked him if he knew why the pair had been so cautious. He told us rather sadly that he had, in fact, repeated his warning just before he left that he would know if she was two-timing him and what the consequences would be. Of course, all that this warning had accomplished was to make the case more difficult and cost him more money. Or maybe, as we tend to suspect on many occasions, with so many of our clients, Rob did not want to know the truth. Perhaps subconsciously, he gave her that warning so she could cover her tracks. Then, in his own mind, her being cautious was tantamount to her being innocent. Yes, human nature can be weird.

This thought was all but confirmed a week later when we gave Rob a final call to verify that he had received the DVD and all the relevant information that had been sent. He told us he had already confronted Ying about her companion, and she had told him it was just her brother's friend staying there until he could find a place of his own. And in any case, the fellow was gay! Amazingly, Rob told us that he believed her! Well, why not: perhaps there is an unwritten Thai law that gay friends of brothers don't have to leave their shoes at the door and are not permitted to leave an apartment the same time as a female?

Thinking of Rob, his trade, and the association with Chiang Mai brings back memories of a case I conducted myself a number of years ago. Allow me to backtrack a little, for this is a good tale that begs to be told.

Over the years, both myself and the current team have uncovered boiler rooms in Bangkok; had almost daily reports of Nigerian 419 scams; been asked to try and retrieve money from numerous versions of the fake-money-in-a-suitcase scam, jewellery scams, the new-suit scam, and just straight-out, basic rip-offs. I thought I had seen them all, but what I have to relate here was, in my opinion, one of the more ingenious.

I had been contacted by a well-known British insurance company that was trying to confirm the value of a supposedly rare, expensive carved teak tiger that they believed came from the Southeast Asian region. A client of the company had purchased the item from an equally well-known UK auction house for a very substantial sum and wished to insure it accordingly.

As is standard operating procedure, the insurance company had their own assessors and investigators check on the background details, and they had noted some discrepancies in the information the original seller of the antique carving had given the auction house at the time of sale to their client. Briefly, the story given by the seller was that he had inherited the item from an old uncle who had apparently spent a lifetime serving in the British army. Included in old uncle's career had been a stint in India during the 1930s, upholding law, order and the British way amongst the colonials. During this time, uncle had attained the rank of Major. (Shades of "It Ain't Half Hot", the British comedy series set in that era, sprang to mind.) According to the seller, his uncle had been given the item by a local maharajah as a token of goodwill. For all these tangled reasons, the seller himself was unable to provide a specific date or place of origin for the prized and intricately carved life-sized teak tiger.

The insurance company was aware that the general rule of thumb regarding any such gifts to officers of Her Majesty's (or, as in that period, His Majesty's) armed forces was that they became gifts to the crown or the state. The insurance people then did a search of their substantial databases and found no trace of any army officer, with major's rank or otherwise, within the seller's immediate family.

This discrepancy had then prompted their investigators to dig a little deeper. I wasn't privy to the company's methods or contacts but simply informed that it "had come to their attention" that not too long before the article was sent to the auction house, the seller had made a reasonable payment to a Chiang Mai-based export company. The insurers asked me to follow up on that particular lead. I rang the Chiang Mai company, said I was buying some teak furniture in the area, and would they be able to arrange shipping to the UK for me. I was assured this was no problem, and that they were very used to handling that type of operation. I mentioned I might buy some additional items as well, and that I was interested in larger teak carvings; could they recommend any companies that specialized in that field. I also added the magic words, "money no problem".

I was given the name of an obviously Thai-Chinese company, based on the outskirts of Chiang Mai, which, I was informed, was renowned for its workmanship and expertise with teak. The insurance company people were not paying any massive retainer, but they were keen to have some further investigation done. As it was early days in the Thai Private Eye business, and clients were not beating down my door at the time, I found myself on the overnight "rattler" to Chiang Mai the following evening. It was 14 bone-shaking hours later, and close to mid-day, when I wandered down the platform of the Chiang Mai station, to be met by a horde of taxi and tuk-tuk drivers, all ready, willing and able to take me to the esteemed company's premises. (Tuk-tuks are three-wheeled, motorcycle-like vehicles that are a popular form of transportation throughout the Kingdom.)

Quotes of 800 baht, then 500 baht soon worked their down to a realistic 150 baht after I had called a few of them thieving lizards in Thai. While Thai is spoken throughout the whole country, most regions also have a local dialect that tends to be used amongst the lower classes, and although I had a decent knowledge of I-san or Lao, as used in the Northeast, and Khamen, as often spoken in those provinces bordering Cambodia, my knowledge of Lanna, the Northern dialect, was pretty much limited to "hello", "good bye" and "how much"!

Most taxi or the tuk-tuk drivers are, in any case, usually happy to take tourists to manufacturing outlets (or yes, massage parlours) on the cheap as they normally get a 10 % payback on any money customers they deliver spend at that particular establishment. A 15-minute ride later, I was walking into the company office and being greeted by a plump, bespectacled, but very pleasant Thai-Chinese woman who spoke near perfect English. As most Thais would tell you, her English abilities, combined with her healthy size, signified she probably came from an affluent family.

This was confirmed a few moments later, after I explained I was an agent buying artefacts for a wealthy client. I, of course, once again mentioned those magic words – "money no problem" – and was duly granted the privilege of having the factory manager come out to give me a personal tour. Obviously a brother of the receptionist, he would have to rely on the heavy gold chain and amulet around his neck rather than his natural good looks to woo one of the region's beauties. As this was a family-run concern, I wouldn't have been at all surprised if mum and dad were not out in the backroom, tools in hand, working on teak!

I was soon to get the chance to find out – or at least to see the actual workroom. I was shown some exquisite pieces in the main showroom, highly lacquered teak tables inlaid with intricate designs, mainly picturing early Thai or Chinese scenes. I knew these were both very expensive and a type of status symbol amongst the Kingdom's wealthier subjects. I passed on my admiration of the work, and mentioned that, as my client was a Westerner, he was more interested in carved teak animals. No problem; I was taken to another part of the showroom, where an array of beautifully crafted birds, monkeys, elephants and, in fact, practically all of the Chinese zodiac signs were on display.

One of the first things I had committed to memory when I became domiciled in Asia was the Chinese zodiac signs. This was for very practical reasons: if you ask the age of an Asian girl, especially one who hangs out in somewhat dubious surroundings, I figure you have a rather slim hope of getting a true answer. Ask her what sign she was born under, however, and invariably you will get the truth. Know your relevant Chinese zodiac dates then, and it becomes "elementary, my dear Watson" as to confirming someone's age – well, at least within a 12-year cycle!

Picking up a shiny black teak horse, a sign I had some affinity with (coincidentally, the horse later became the sign my daughter was born under), I told my very obliging guide that my client was born in 1950, and I wondered what sign that was. "Ah, that is tiger," he said, confirming what I already knew. This neatly led to my next question: "Have you ever made life-sized tigers?"

I was again told "no ploblem", and, in fact, that type of request was relatively common, but as they were made to order, he did not have any on hand to show me. The only life-sized larger animals currently in the store were the elephants at the showroom entrance.

I informed my new friend that my client would be very keen to order a life-sized tiger, and yes, a substantial deposit was, likewise, no problem. This was becoming very much a "no-problem" investigation. However, the big query was yet to come. I told him the only thing working against his company's obviously high quality, top-class works of art was the fact that my client was a great collector of antiques, and his first preference, if possible, would be to purchase a life-sized teak tiger that had perhaps been made many years ago. Guess what: I drew a knowing smile, followed by yet another "no ploblem"

I was duly escorted to the rear of the showroom, a door was unlocked, and I was ushered into what was, in fact, a huge workshop. The workers here were mostly women. (Whether or not the manager's mother was amongst them, I'm not sure.) All had their heads down and were hard at work on various stages of a vast array of products.

There was a strong odour present, intensified by a lack of air vents, which wouldn't have pleased Western health authorities.

I assumed it came from the lacquer coating being applied. I was soon to find out that this assumption was incorrect.

Mr Manager led me towards the rear of the large building and opened what seemed to be a small drying cabinet. He carefully lifted out an object and handed me the most intricate, delicate piece of woodwork I had ever seen: a very finely carved sea horse. I took it gingerly, afraid of damaging such an aged and fragile piece. "Beautiful," I told him. "How old is it?"

"What you think?" he asked me.

Having absolutely no idea, I guessed, "Fifty years at least."

Again, I got that knowing smile. I gently handed the carving back, he returned it to the cabinet, and beckoned me towards a large vat at the very rear of the workshop. "Sea horse we make last week," he told me, as I gazed at a number of pieces of teak floating in an open, very toxic-smelling vat of acid! "Soak in here a few days, make look very old"

"*Khon Jeen chalart mark*" was all I could say, letting him know in Thai that Chinese people were indeed very clever. (Although born and bred Thais, those with a Chinese heritage still adhere closely to their Chinese roots and are happy to be referred to as "*Khon Jeen*", or Chinese person.)

This compliment was again met with a nod and a smile. The tour was over, and my guide keen to leave the workroom, the acid fumes making his bespectacled eyes blink profusely.

"You can treat a life-sized tiger this way?" I asked.

"No ploblem, we make tiger many time, even make real-size elephant this style," he boasted.

"That will be perfect for my client then," I told him. "I will confirm the order first thing tomorrow."

As he turned to lead the way out, I slipped a small camera out of my pocket and, aware of the numerous camera signs around with a large red cross over them, quickly snapped off some shots while following him back to the refreshing, air-cooled showroom.

They were not the greatest of prints, but along with my report, they certainly gave a much more accurate indication of the formerly unknown origin and year of manufacture of the teak tiger that had recently been sold at auction over in the UK for a very substantial sum.

The insurance company expressed their thanks, and told me they would be certain to contact us regarding any future Asian investigations. Just what the result of my investigation was, I never did find out, although no doubt the request for a very substantial insurance cover was dismissed.

I do sympathize with the person buying what he or she believed was a genuine antique. Nevertheless, I had to admit it was indeed a well-worked scam, and it further bolstered the solid attitude I have developed over the years: with regard to investigations in Asia, and the subsequent results of these investigations, nothing, but NOTHING, surprises me!

QUEEN TO PAWN 1 – CHECKMATE

"The House always wins."
Las Vegas maxim

Once again, it had appeared to be a fairly straightforward case. Okay, a straightforward needle-in-a-haystack case, but the type we get on a surprisingly regular basis. Knowing I had been involved in this type of scenario many times, the appointed case control officer gave me a quick call and asked for a few suggestions. He noted it was the type of case where his area of expertise – surveillance technology, listening, tracking, shooting videos – did not appear to be of much use. He was to be proven very wrong in that respect, but that was all to come later.

Martin had called the company after we had been recommended by a friend of his who had used our services not long before. An American, Martin was domiciled in Kuwait. Although we never asked, and he never volunteered the information, it was more than likely he was perhaps there on behalf of Uncle Sam. We did learn he was middle-aged, presentable, single, and well-off!

As a number of his compatriots have done over the years, he often spent his R&R in the Land of Smiles. The network of US expats is pretty strong in Bangkok, and getting good advice on where to go, who to ask for, and how much to pay is all readily available. Martin was a Thai girl's dream in a number of ways – American, unattached, good job and not tight with his money – but up till then, he had avoided the pitfalls of a permanent relationship with a Thai lass; not that he was averse to them in any way. He had the usual little black book full of Thai mobile numbers and a sprinkling of demimondaines' email addresses he had bothered to keep. Hence, it was not usually any problem to have a friendly acquaintance knocking on his hotel door shortly after he had checked in to his normal haunt, the Landmark, a better-class hotel. For his wants and needs, the Landmark was ideally located close to both Nana Plaza and the many nefarious Sukhumvit Road watering holes.

Martin asked if we could perhaps drop by the Landmark and have a chat. Not our usual procedure, but as he was guaranteed by a former good client and he stressed that it was an urgent matter, we made an exception.

He explained to the appointed case controller that he had been in the downstairs pub of the Landmark, a fairly high-class establishment as far as watering holes in that area go. A Thai girl had been sitting nearby for some time, gazing blankly at an empty bottle of Singha Beer. He had asked her if she would like a refill, and thus he had come to meet Ree. He had sensed something of himself in Miss Ree (short for her full name, Areerat, she had told him), who it seemed was something of a loner and a bit of a lost soul. She was 26, dressed in designer jeans and T-shirt, no make-up, obviously not desperate to find a provider for the night, and said she was actually just waiting for her friend, who had a short time before gone upstairs to visit someone.

Her English was not too bad, she admitted to some time in Singapore and Malaysia, and quite refreshingly didn't have tales of a sick grandmother's dying buffalo or numerous siblings to support. Over the next few hours, and a number of drinks, Martin learnt she had two older brothers – one a builder, one in the army – her parents had a small banana plantation in Ratchaburi, and she had come to Bangkok about a year ago to complete a hairdressing course. She also admitted to Martin that she sometimes forgot to attend said course.

They had ended up spending the remainder of his sojourn together, and Martin, even with his extensive experience with Thai ladies of the night, admitted he was completely smitten with the demure Miss Ree, her perfect body, and her remarkable prowess between the sheets!

They spent most of the remainder of his stay together. Some new clothes, meals, and an ample supply of drinks was all he was asked for, which, not surprisingly, endeared her to him even more.

There were no demands for money, no disappearing at odd hours to satisfy husbands or other sponsors, no secretive phone calls. What's more, Ree had an easy-going attitude and was happy to go wherever or do whatever Martin wanted. In other words, she was the ideal companion, and he was about ready to throw his little black book of other contacts into the rubbish bin. He bought her a gold bracelet and had to force US$1,000 into the back pocket of her designer jeans on the day he had to sadly return to Kuwait. And that wasn't just because they were so tight-fitting!

Back at work, Martin called her almost daily. On a couple of occasions she had sounded drunk, but said the reason was that she was sad and missed him. At other times, there was talk in the background, just her roommates playing cards supposedly, and, in fact, she had put some of them on the phone. All seemed fine then, and there was even talk of a trip to meet her family in Ratchaburi.

It was only two days before he was due to return to Bangkok that suddenly all contact was lost. The adage that absence makes the heart grow fonder had become quite pertinent in Martin's case: he was really looking forward to his return and wondering if, in fact, this relationship might well develop into something more permanent.

He realized there was no doubt a lot about Ree he didn't know, and obviously she had some "skeletons in the closet". She did get depressed at times, often tried to drown her sorrows, and he figured the local *yaa baa* form of methamphetamine was something that she probably was not a complete stranger to. However, he still found it hard to fathom why she was suddenly incommunicado.

The only point of contact he had, apart from her mobile phone which now gave a recorded message in Thai saying the number was no longer operative, was the room she told him she shared at a well- known, dilapidated and definitely dodgy Phetchburi Road apartment block. He had taken her there one time to get some clothes, and, perhaps as he was trained to do in such circumstances, had made a note of the building name and room number.

He remembered a rather grandiose name, not entirely fitting for the large apartment blocks grouped together that house hundreds of bargirls, karaoke and massage parlour workers, along with Nigerian scammers, hard-up English teachers and assorted other hangers-on and wannabes. It had been late evening when Martin arrived back in Bangkok, so he had gone straight to the apartment block. After a little trial and error, he had found room 616. However, the door was locked, and there was no sign of life. He had returned the next morning and managed to rouse a couple of sleepy Thai girls in the room who would only say "Ree gone" and made it clear that was the end of the conversation. It was at this stage that Martin had called us and asked help in finding his missing love.

Allowing that he really knew little of her background and had even less to go on as to her possible whereabouts, he understood Miss Ree might well be a lost cause, in more ways than one. However, Martin was not short of money and he didn't like unsolved mysteries. Perhaps he had just met her when she was between sponsors, or had had an argument with her husband; a slew of possibilities suggested themselves. However, he felt he knew her well enough that these were not too likely, or else she was a very good actor. He also worried that something more serious may have happened to her and felt he at least owed it to her, and himself, to try and delve a little deeper into her disappearance.

The Phetchburi Road apartments seemed the only lead, so that's where, the following day, two of our agents headed in search of Room 616 and some possible answers. Agent #1 in this case was one of our best Thai female operatives. Some years back, she had had a sponsor or two herself; however, these days she was happily married to one of our staff. With training, she had adapted remarkably to the investigative role, and her understanding of many situations from the Thai female perspective was often invaluable.

As a cover story, a Western Union sticker was placed on her jacket and some of the company's forms put on a clipboard that she carried in a shoulder bag along with a video cam. She also had a recording device and a buttonhole cam: quite the walking advert for high tech equipment.

Agent #2, in the guise of her motorcycle taxi driver, set off with her to the apartment block, which was well known to us from various investigations over the years. We never send an agent out alone and always try to have a plausible cover story for them. Of course, we knew that Western Union is not in the door-to-door delivery business, but this is a ruse that Thais of the background we were dealing with would not question, especially if money was purportedly headed for someone in their group! They soon found their way to room 616. Shoes outside the door and some muffled sounds from within that a small sound amplifier the size of a pack of cigarettes held briefly and carefully against the door, identified as small talk and card shuffling confirmed that the room was certainly occupied now.

Unusually, however, the door was shut, a careful turn on the doorknob signified it was locked, and even the cockroach entry under the doorway had been blocked by a towel. In those type of apartments, where humidity is high and air-conditioners rare, it is normal for Thai occupants who are at home and awake to leave the door and windows open to help air circulate. Locking the door and blocking it tends to signify those within are probably up to no good! Perhaps just playing cards for money, which although it comes in only slightly behind eating and TV watching as favourite Thai pastimes, still happens to be illegal. (This, incidentally, is a law that has proved a boon for the boys in brown, the Thai police uniform colour, as any time they uncover a game, they can automatically confiscate any monies found on the premises!)

Although games are often played for a few baht, stakes can, of course, climb much higher in what is normally a form of poker. Another reason for secrecy, and perhaps even more common in these dodgy apartments, is that drugs are present in the room.

After much whispering and shuffling, the door was finally opened a fraction. Agent #1 pointed to her Western Union stuck-on logo, waved her clipboard, and said she had a contact notice for room 616. We were safe to assume that some, if not all those present, would have at some time received payments via the international money transfer agents. And, of course, any mention of money opens doors in most places, especially Bangkok. Given that slight opening, our agent was quickly inside. She deftly placed her camera-carrying bag on a table, making sure it was directed at the five or six girls still sitting in a semi-circle on the floor.

She then consulted her clipboard and asked for Miss Areerat – only to be told she was not there. But the room's owner, who gave her name as Mam, assured our agent that she could represent her "relation". Mam, late fifties, dripping with gold, and sporting blonde streaks in her hair that looked like they had been applied by a blind man with a paintbrush, was obviously in charge of the group. Just as clearly, she was a former lady of the night herself, who, like many of her ilk, didn't realize, or admit to knowing, that she was well past her sell-by date.

Not missing a beat, Agent #1 then asked for some ID. She

noted Mam's details, which she wisely figured might come in handy, and explained the reason for her visit, saying the sender had paid an extra fee to confirm the address of the person receiving the money. She said this also involved reminding the beneficiary that if the money was not collected personally within a week, the funds would be returned to the sender.

"We normally phone," she told Mam, "but the number we were given seems out of order." Mam assured her she would try and get the message to Areerat, and made it clear the conversation was over. Picking up her bag, our agent quickly left the building with Agent #2 before those in the card game had any second thoughts.

Agents #1 and #2 were then stood down from the assignment, and agents #3 and #4 brought into the office. Middle-aged Thai men, one doubled as a taxi driver, the other had been a fairly handy kick-boxer in his day; in fact, he was still handy in the present day! They both sat down with the appointed case controller and watched the video of the girls in the room over and over, along with descriptions given by the previous two agents.

A set of reasonable pictures was made and transferred to their mobile phones, and they were then sent to spend the rest of the day (and night, if need be) eating and drinking at the tables scattered outside the small food-stalls that served the inhabitants of the dingy apartments. Their task was to identify one of the girls from room 616, preferably one who appeared to perhaps have lost her money or been sent out as the lowly food collector.

Apart from Mam, it was probable that most of those present when our agent visited would be susceptible to a little pressure and some money and would then perhaps divulge more about Ree's disappearance. Our female agent, who was not often wrong in such situations, believed Ms Mam was hiding a lot more than she was letting on.

Control had meanwhile updated the client and asked him to go to the nearest Western Union office and send his beloved a small amount, but to make sure the transaction was tracked, an often useful service offered by the money transfer company, as it provides a way to check a girl's whereabouts. The sender is then able to log on and find out when and where a payment is collected.

Meanwhile, our agents had settled down to some snack food and chat outside the apartments. It was not too many hours later that an opportunity arose: an elderly Thai lady, wheeling a trolley and ringing a small bell, wandered up the alleyway between the apartment blocks, and our agents identified a girl from the video who was approaching the hawker. She went to purchase some grasshoppers fried in oil, a favourite amongst many Thais. Noting that the young lady only bought a small amount and used loose change rather than notes to pay, our agents decided the girl seemed a likely candidate for bribing, so when she took her small bag of food and headed slowly towards another of the dingy blocks, the agents casually followed here.

Agent #3 was able to get in the lift with the target, and saw her press Level 4, so he pressed Level 2 for himself and quickly text-messaged a "Four" to his co-agent, who was already in the building stairwell. Our man in the lift then cursed loudly that he had made a mistake with Floor 2, he really wanted Floor 3. Having already slowed the lift down, he then bent over in the lift doorway when it reached the 3rd floor, spending a moment to do up his shoelace – and also to have a good look at the girl's footwear. By the time the lift finally reached Level 4, our second agent was sitting on the window ledge at the end of the hallway, apparently having a somewhat heated discussion with his wife on his mobile phone which in actual fact was off, although the video camera therein was certainly on.

The hallway lighting was not great, but certainly good enough to identify the subject and see her take her shoes off, shoes the agent from the lift was also able to confirm as hers. There were no other shoes outside at that point. More important for our team, she had used a key to open the door to Apartment 402 rather than knocking. It did indeed seem that she was on her own, so the agents called into Control with an update on the situation and suggested it might be just the time to take a chance and call on her.

Control gave me a quick call, reminding me that these days, impersonating various officials is much more of a no-no. After some discussion, knowing most girls in those apartments don't spend much time in rooms alone, we decided to approach her immediately.

The simplest plan was then to have our Thai agents basically tell the truth. No need to mention who had engaged them, but just say that they had been hired to track down Ree, and were able to offer a reward for helpful information; said information would, of course, remain strictly confidential. As a month's rent at the apartments is around 5000 baht, that was the sum we decided to offer if the girl could indeed shed any light on the subject.

It was almost midnight when Agent #3, toting a few cans of beer, and agent #4, prominently displaying five crisp, white 1,000-baht notes, knocked on the door of Apartment 402. A few moments later, they were greeted by the somewhat bloodshot eyes of a rather plain and tired-looking Thai girl who, they estimated, was in her late twenties. She peered at them through the gap of the door held by a safety chain.

Thai women on their own, especially in these apartments, are not in any hurry to allow men into their rooms, so the money and beer were quickly produced and a calm and quiet explanation of what they were interested in was given.

The money was waved: "This is for just having a little chat with us" they said, whilst swearing they were not police but investigators just making some simple enquiries, and anything she told them would be kept totally confidential. As she hesitated, they continued to wave the money. Finally, the safety chain was unhooked and a girl who gave her name as "Gay" (although seemingly anything but) cautiously beckoned them in.

It took some time, and another trip downstairs for some food and more beer, before they made real progress. Our agents do not generally drink on the job, but it is part of Thai culture that food and drink go together with any lengthy conversation. It had quickly become apparent that their approach to Gay had been timely: not only was she broke and desperate, but she did have useful information to pass on as well. To keep the conversation rolling along as smoothly as was the small digital voice recorder Agent # 3 had casually placed on the table, extra drink and an extra 1000 baht note were offered ... and quickly accepted.

All our agents are instructed in effective interview or interrogation procedures. It is, in fact, a field I personally specialize in these days. It is amazing just how much personal and often unsolicited information you can obtain by asking open-ended questions, usually about side issues such as family or hometown, by not interrupting and giving the subjects as long as they want to talk or answer. Having a good supply of food and drink on hand also helps in these procedures.

We were lucky on this occasion. Gay proved to be the ideal choice: she was desperate, under a lot of pressure, and had no one to talk to. The agents had to listen to her own problems first, listen to her justify in her own mind taking the money and passing on information, but they had been taught that by being patient, generally the truth will out.

Gay told them she was four months pregnant and no longer went to work at a popular bar and pool room where she had met her Swiss boyfriend almost a year earlier. When she became pregnant, the boyfriend had asked her to stay home and rest, and he sent her plenty of money for food and rent each month while he was, for the time being, hard at work back in the land of the watchmakers. It was obvious that most of the money went to card games, as there was very little food in the room, and Gay was quick to eat the snack food provided.

Gay then asked one of those vague questions that perhaps only a Thai girl being in the company of apparently wise and knowledgeable investigators would ask. "Can you test for a baby's colour?" This is what I mean by letting a subject chat away and all sorts of information can surface! Reassured everything discussed was totally confidential, Gay mentioned that around the time she became pregnant, there had been an occasion with one of the Thai motorcycle taxi riders who she had an on-again-off-again affair with for years. In addition to that dalliance, when very drunk one night, having lost the month's rent money playing cards, she had ventured into the room of a nice Nigerian man downstairs. Whether the baby would be fair, olive or dark-skinned, seemed to be very much in question! Perhaps we would be getting a call from Switzerland in five months time!

Gay certainly had her own problems. Gradually, however, with some more food and beer, the conversation was carefully steered around to Ree and her mysterious disappearance. Backing up Martin's testimony, Gay told them Ree did not have any close friends or family. She knew her from playing cards together in Mam's room and was also sure that Ree and Mam sometimes did some sort of business together. What followed then was quite a tale, and certainly altered the course, degree of difficulty, and the danger of finding Martin's lost love.

What the agents related when back at the office, confirmed with the tape recording, was the following: Mam, the older woman from Room 616, nowadays made her money mostly by introducing younger girls from upcountry to various bars and massage parlours around the city. She also acted as a go-between for a Malay syndicate which ran various activities in Thailand, Singapore and Malaysia. These, we came to learn, included illicit casino operations, along with the usual sidelines: a ready supply of drugs, prostitution and pornography.

Gay hadn't known Mam all that long, but understood Ree was perhaps one of her earlier inductees into this type of lifestyle. Gay herself had only met Ree recently, after she had apparently returned from a three-month spell at Singapore's well-known night-time haunt, Orchard Towers. Gay then went on to relate how Ree had told her she made a lot of money in Singapore, although it was also clear that the biggest part of this had been absorbed by agent's fees, commissions, and, of course, drugs, to which Ree was apparently addicted. She still, however, had enough money left to go often with Mam to the "casino", as Gay called it.

These "casinos" are normally just a house or apartment where various card games and other forms of gambling are run illicitly. Gay had been there once or twice when she had money and knew it was in the Suttisan district, about a 30-minute taxi trip away, but she did not recall exactly where. In any case, being an illegal den, apparently backed by Malaysian interests, it would be well-protected one way or another. Without the means to gamble "big time", the girls would play for small amounts in Mam's apartment. Ree had soon lost her earnings but had recently come into money again – no doubt, Martin's parting gift. That had allowed Ree to again accompany Mam to the "casino", where she had soon lost her latest windfall as well.

Gay's narrative then got very interesting: As she now had boasted of a "rich sponsor" and also was happy to work in Singapore or Malaysia, it was easy for Ree to gamble at the casino on credit, Gay mentioned. She had heard Ree was now in debt to the syndicate. Obviously too embarrassed to ask, or even unsure if Martin would bail her out, Ree apparently learned that the syndicate were about to make a new run of pornographic movies and had asked Mam to find some suitable actors. Mam had put forward a distant relation from her own village who was very pretty but also drug-addicted and in dire need of money. Now, with the set-up complete, they had Ree available to make up the duet.

The pair had travelled south by train a few days previously and were now in Malaysia. Gay knew this for sure, as the girls had called Mam earlier in the day, when Gay herself was there playing cards, to say they had arrived and were okay. They had mentioned they were staying at a nice hotel and expected to be back in a week or so, well cashed up! As far as Gay could recall, contact details, or at least a phone number that Mam had written down on the back of a playing card was behind a fridge magnet in room 616.

Following the agents' debriefing, Martin was contacted, and we discussed what further action could be taken. Our initial thought was to offer Gay another payment, then return to Mam's apartment and get the contact information. If the phone number there was indeed a Malaysian landline, we could soon track down the location. That, of course, would not be of much help, especially if it was a secure room. What's more, previous escapades south of the Thai border had alerted me to the fact that corruption and the carrying of guns were widespread there, especially in certain provinces. But Martin assured us that now he had started, he wanted to see this thing through. He was incensed to learn that this sweet young girl he was infatuated with had perhaps been forced into making pornographic movies. It had become something of a personal mission for him to right any wrong.

We agreed to see if Gay could get us the number and to look at further options if she was successful. Gay was then asked to do so. Upon being told it would involve a nice bonus for her, she assured us it would be no problem. Loyalty is generally not a strong suit amongst Thai girls, or at least those women working in the night trades.

It is always a problem using people in this manner, and something we try to avoid if possible. When we need to rely upon a usually nervous and untrained person, it often seems that if something can go wrong, it will. But in this case, we had little choice, as Martin was pressing us and time was tight. But his time we were lucky. Whether it was desperation for the bonus or the fact that, as Gay had told us, Ree was always nice to her whereas Mam looked down on her, we're not sure. But in any event, Gay's resolve in this instance held, and by the following evening, we had a phone number.

Our next call was to a friendly investigation agency in Malaysia. The old-boy network is fairly strong and healthy amongst respected investigation companies world-wide. Our colleagues quickly pinpointed the phone's location: a reasonably well-known hotel in the city of Ipoh. Further, they came up with an extension number, which was more than likely the room number.

Their added information, however, was not so encouraging, although they did confirm that we were probably on the right track. The hotel was well known as being a legal business that was actually owned and operated by a group whose core activities were anything but legal. What's more, a number of pornographic movies certainly had been shot in and around the hotel. Its impressive foyer, Chinese banquet hall, and outdoor pool often featured in scenes of low-class, underground movies.

Our associates further pointed out that since these Malaysian gangsters were now operating on their home turf (the hotel they owned), they would probably feel rather secure. For this reason, they most likely would not have seen any cause to monitor the Thai "starlets" too closely. More, the girls would be unlikely to have any ID, money or passports on them, so they could not go far. The hotel, they said, had security cameras and was some distance from the local airport, shops, and the central district of Ipoh.

It was then time for some serious decisions all round. Martin had to decide whether or not he wanted us to continue the investigation, as, with the travel and agents involved, it was about to become an expensive operation. If he did wish to locate Ree, we had to decide how far we would go. We won't unnecessarily endanger any of our operatives, and this now bore the hallmarks of a potentially very dangerous assignment.

But Martin was hooked. He assured us Ree deserved a chance,

and he was particularly upset over the way she had, he believed, been conned out of her money and forced into the position she was in. He understood we could not charge in like an anti-terrorist squad and also that contacting the authorities was going to be of little help. However, he wanted us to do all we could, to at least try and contact the girl and let her know help was nearby. And then he lathered on that wonderful salve: money was no object.

In the end, we settled on a compromise. We would send our best male and female agents south to check into the hotel and try to locate Ree. Step Two would be to try to speak to her on her own, which is why we needed a female, as perhaps a "chance encounter" in a ladies toilet would offer the best opportunity. If we could get this far and verify that Ree was being detained against her will, we would then work on a plan for the agents to try and discreetly spirit her away from the hotel. Or, if Ree preferred, we could at least slip her some money to help her make her own escape.

Our agreement was that, should we find her, we would explain that Martin was very worried about her and had asked us to do all we could to reunite them. We stipulated, however, that our agents would not confront any men who might be guarding Ree, and we would not allow the agents to be put in any position where they, or Ree, might be threatened.

That was as far as we could go. Martin seemed happy with that. He did, of course, want to accompany the team south, but that was something we could not agree to. We devised an elaborate escape route for our agents if, by chance, they were able to get Ree into a car covertly, and we assured Martin he would be regularly updated or put in phone contact with her immediately – if that possibility eventuated.

Even assuming our agents were not only able to locate the missing lovely, but also (and I realised this was a very large "BUT") escort her safely and secretly out of Ipoh, that would not be the end of our problems. Knowing the way things work around that area, we also had to assume that there could well be those at Ipoh airport and the main Malaysian border crossing to Thailand at Padeng Bazzar who were in the pay of the syndicate. We therefore needed to remain extremely discreet throughout the entire operation. My strategy was not to fly our agents directly to Ipoh, but into Kuala Lumpur, and for them to hire a vehicle there and drive the 200 kilometres up to Ipoh. We would also have our Malaysian counterparts on standby if needed, although Martin was understandably against any additional involvement.

Once in Malaysia, we needed our people to remain covert and free from suspicion for as long as possible. If they were able to locate Ree and arrange to have her moved unnoticed from the hotel, and into their rental car, my plan was for them to then drive another 200 kilometres up the coast to the small seaside town of Alor Setar. From there, they could take a ferry to the nearby island resort of Langkawi, the most northern island in Malaysian waters. From Langkawi, a ferry (of which there are four or five each day) lands you in the southern Thai town of Satun in just over an hour's time. Being Thai, Ree would only need a Thai ID card, of which our agents had extras, to get herself on the ferry and back on Thai soil.

That, then, was the simple plan. But, of course, carrying it all out would be anything but simple. Flights to Kuala Lumpur depart Bangkok on the hour, so that helped, and it is a fairly straightforward drive up Malaysia's expansive central highway from KL to Ipoh, a city that owed its existence mainly to tin mining.

It was late in the evening when our two agents arrived at the hotel and went to a rather busy coffee shop and general meeting place just inside the entrance. They discussed their chances of finding what floor the movie-makers might be on and the best way to get a room nearby. The extension number given to the hotel phone number was 903, and a look at the hotel brochure had confirmed it was indeed a nine-storey building.

We had thought earlier of just calling the number, and the room, but we felt that would do little but endanger the operation and possibly put the syndicate on the alert. Being discreet was, we felt, the key to success in this investigation especially. Also, it was obvious that even if the girls were in the room, they would be unlikely to answer the phone themselves. Being a former British colony, many Malaysians speak good English. However, they also speak their own mother tongues when together, and that was yet another problem we would face.

Fortified by a coffee, our agents decided to go straight to the core of the problem, or at least to try and verify it. Accordingly, they ventured over to the hotel lift, pressed the 9th floor button, and headed upwards. Using an old, but as is often the case, good technique, they staggered out of the lift, looking like a rather drunk and confused couple trying to find their room. This proved to be wise strategy. Just past the elevator entrance, a white chain hung across the hallway, with a "Private – no admittance" sign attached. Apparently, there were only six large suites on that floor, and the agents could make out that the doors of Rooms 903 and 904, sitting opposite, both seemed to be open, and from the sounds emanating out, a party (or was that an orgy) seemed to be in full swing. The chance of getting any closer, however, was curtailed by a menacing-looking guy who sat at a small desk just inside the chained-off area, and said simply, "Private; you go now."

Our pair could do little but get back into the lift and go down to reception. There, they asked for a top floor suite, only to be told that none were available at the moment; fancy that. It had been a long day, so they checked into a room on the floor below, updated the case controller, and left it to him to figure out the next move.

We wondered if our Malaysian agency backup might be able

to place staff quickly in the hotel to "cover for a sick housemaid", but that was clutching at straws. Martin was kept in the loop, and he certainly did not want to go down that path. As he pointed out, it was not so much the additional expense, or the time it would take to get them on board, but, confirming that he had certainly done his homework on the region, we needed to keep activities around Ipoh strictly amongst ourselves to avoid any chance of the investigation being compromised.

Considering that much of the criminal activity in that area was related to Chinese-Malay syndicates with known triad links, we had to agree. But we also had to come up with some novel – and quick – approach to try and confirm whether or not Ree was indeed amongst the occupants of the top floor suites.

Martin was very keen to get some video or photographic evidence, but we struggled to come up with a feasible plan that would not endanger our agents or compromise the mission. Placing any sort of snake, web, or video cam anywhere on the top floor, which we now knew sported a 24-hour guard, was not going to be a simple matter. Security cameras, the agents had noted, also covered most of the hotel, both inside and out. The case controller had, of course, included what he could in their travel kit in the way of surveillance equipment, and, as a cover, we provided paperwork saying they were salespeople in this field. Even so, travelling across national borders meant they were somewhat restricted technologically.

In the end, we opted to go once again with one of my old tried-and-true methods for covertly moving a substance or placing an object elsewhere. Well, one I had borrowed from Asians, if you want to be exact.

First thing the next morning, we sent our agents off for shopping at the city's largest mall. As it happened, Easter was fast approaching, so chocolate Easter eggs and bunnies were out in force. The agents brought the largest stuffed bunny they could find; that it happened to be holding a basket containing Easter eggs was going to be a bonus for the occupants of the 9th floor. The bugging operation was carried out by our female agent, who placed a small listening device behind the bunny's eye, where it would not attract attention.

Many bugging devices are commonly available; unfortunately, few work as well as their promoters claim. There are also, of course, many variables, in particular, the power source. Room interference is another common problem, which books or movies dealing with bugging generally ignore. Also, many people will have a TV on when in a room and awake, and this tends to distort feedback. Further, placing a device in a bag or pocket will generally result in muffled sound, and we knew in this case, the rabbit would perhaps need to be on a bed, or at least close to the occupants, to provide much audible *and* understandable conversation. Certainly the best results come from placing a bug in a room's power source or light socket, but in this case, the only two hopes of that, were none and Bob!

There is one other small matter here: discreetly recording other people's conversations is an offence punishable by law, which is another reason for being particularly careful in how you plan this type of operation. In this instance, however, included in our agents' bag of goodies was a small Israeli-made FM transmitter type device. This device was roughly the size of the bunny's eyeball, and we knew it would work well, even through walls, for a distance of 100 to 150 meters. However, there was a drawback with this type of device: the only power source we could use was an equally small battery, and again we knew from experience that this would only last about four or five hours. Nonetheless, it was the best instrument we could come up with, considering all the circumstances. Anyway, at this point, we were only trying to confirm that Ree was actually in the room. So we set ourselves to performing a little eye surgery.

Whilst the rabbit was on the operating table, our other agent ran out and picked up some wrapping paper. Shortly thereafter, the gift was ready. A card with "Room 902 " written on it was then duly placed on top of the basket of eggs. They squeezed Bugs Bunny, as he had now been fittingly dubbed, into a large plastic bag and drove to the airport, our girl behind the wheel. She dropped her partner off, along with Bugs, and he quickly strode into the building, then back out to the waiting taxi rank. Picking out an older driver, who he hoped had no young children who would love a large white bunny holding a basket of Easter eggs, he asked how much the fare to the hotel was, then handed over double, saying he was running late, but could the driver deliver the bunny in the bag to the hotel reception area and tell them it was for room 902.

He watched the taxi drive off, trusting the driver would carry out his instructions, and then went back to find his fellow agent, relatively happy that their cover remained safe. As to getting some audio from Room 902, well, that would be in the lap of the gods – or, in this case, in the eye of the bunny.

Asian women of all ages tend to have a childlike affinity for stuffed animals, so that, coupled with the fact that Easter was approaching and the hope that some of the guys in the suite might have had an interest in the girls staying content, we felt we had a 50-50 chance of Bugs being allowed into the inner sanctum of the hotel's top floor.

Of course, what was also required, should our Trojan bunny be accepted, was that it be placed in an area where our agents, back in their room below, could get some idea of just what was happening in the suites above before the battery ran down .

Returning to the hotel, they cast a casual look around the reception area. With no sign of any Easter bunny, they hoped their efforts had reaped a positive result.

Back in their room, the agents tuned in and waited. The sounds of a door shutting and a toilet flushing were the first signs that the plan may just be working. After that, however, silence reigned. Had Bugs been put in a cupboard, or had the battery already run down? It was approaching mid-day when some mumblings were first detected, and shortly thereafter, a clear word that had the agents do a quiet high-five. *Grad-dai*, the Thai word for rabbit, had been clearly heard, which triggered our agents' elation.

One problem for the agents now was that they did not know the actual sound of Ree's voice, so without a visual sighting, we would have to play a copy of the muffled audio feedback to Martin, which we had arranged to do as soon as possible to try and get conformation. However, now our agents were sure that at least two Thai girls were indeed in the suites above.

Snippets of conversation filtered through, mostly female and in Thai, and the one thing that did become apparent was that the occupants were about to go downstairs to eat. This could well be the breakthrough we needed. Our male agent sauntered out into the hallway, looking as though he was waiting for someone, but he was actually keeping an eye on the lifts to see if any went to Level 9, while the female agent continued to monitor the transmitter feedback. Fading voices, followed by a door shutting, signified to her that the subjects were leaving the suite, and a moment later, the outside agent reported the lift heading up past the 8th floor that they were on.

The main hotel restaurant was on the first floor, while the coffee shop and 24-hour snack bar were on the ground floor. There was also the possibility that the party would be going outside to eat. Our agent in the hallway pressed the down button, while the other waited in the room, door ajar, ready to provide back-up. When the lift stopped at the 8th floor, our agent stepped in and joined the lady whom he knew from Martin's photographs to be the elusive Ree. Another slim Thai girl was with her. Both had casual clothes and dark glasses on, and looked like they had had a very hard night!

Accompanying the girls was the surly minder whom the agents had encountered on their earlier visit to the 9th floor. Noting they had pressed the button for the 1st Floor, our man pressed Ground, then quickly punched a numeral 1 into his mobile phone and sent a text message off to his sister agent.

Level 1 housed what was called the Chinese banquet hall, and when our female agent arrived there a few minutes later, *Yum Cha*, the popular Chinese lunch spread was in full swing. She asked for a table for two, and was shown to a place some distance from the group she assumed was their quarry; but they were, nonetheless, within sight. A text to her fellow agent soon had him joining her, and they partook in an impressive array of the usual *Yum Cha* fare of chicken's feet, various dumplings, sticky rice, Peking duck and custard tarts while waiting to see if Miss Ree, whom they were reasonably sure they had now located, might at some point adjourn to the ladies' room.

The table the Thai girls were at now included another five or six people, and judging from the personal waiter service, there was certainly affluence, or at least influence, among the more senior men seated there. Enough glittering bracelets, necklaces and medallions were on show to start a small gold shop, while it was obvious that the array of sunglasses had not been picked up cheaply at a local market. Those shades were evidently needed to cover badly bloodshot eyes.

The body language of the girls did not indicate any sign of worry or being detained, but until we could actually speak to her privately, we would have no idea of Ree's current level of freedom, her itinerary, or, indeed, her state of mind.

Finally, the other girl we assumed was also Thai (as well as a relative of Ms Mam) made a move towards the restroom, and our agents saw that Ree was about to follow. Our female agent moved quickly, and was able to get between the pair, while the other agent continued to watch the table to see if any minders went after the girls. He was relieved to see that conversation and eating seemed to be continuing as before. As the first girl entered the bathroom, our lady agent was able to intercept Ree right at the entrance, telling her in Thai that she needed to speak to her quickly and urgently.

Ree seemed happy enough to hear her out, so she quickly got to the point of the conversation. Was she okay? Was she being held against her will? Did she need help in getting out of Malaysia? Although showing signs of drug use, hangover, and other associated repercussions of an orgy, Ree confirmed that was her name and asked how our agent knew it.

"Oh, I know Mam," was our agent's quick reply, which was accepted with a nod.

"Did she send you?" Ree then asked.

"No. Actually, Martin has been a little worried about you," our agent replied.

"Who is Martin? " was the rather surprising answer our agent got to that admission.

Somewhat knocked off stride by that remark, our agent was contemplating what else to say when Ree's friend poked her head out the door to see where she was. Fortunately, Ree told her all was fine, that she would be there in a minute, then repeated her question. After being told Martin, the American you met last month in Bangkok, the penny dropped, and Ree explained that yes, she did intend to meet him, but suddenly another movie offer had come up and she had to put her career first. This time it was our agent's turn to be somewhat confused: "Career??"

"Oh, yes," Ree enthused, "This is the second movie I make here, and the next one going to be made at Phuket with a German director. He said he's going to make me famous."

Ree told the agent to say "Hi" to her friend Martin, and to tell him she would try and catch up when she was back in Bangkok next week. She then turned and went to join her friend and co-star in the ladies' room.

A somewhat dazed agent made her way back to her partner, and when he asked how it all had gone, she told him he'd better forget that last custard tart, as they should get out of there as soon as possible – just in case Ree mentioned something to her friends, financial supporters, or fans, whatever bracket you might put them in. Moreover, the agents would certainly be travelling on their own as it was now clear that Ree was certainly not under any restraint. In fact, she was rather enjoying her somewhat dubious association with fame and the pornographic film world.

As any interference with their star, or interruption to their schedule, would no doubt not be well received by the syndicate, it was certainly time to depart Ipoh ASAP. As our agents are always prepared for a quick departure, the woman went down to reception to check out while the man quickly returned to the room to pick up their packed bags, gather the audio equipment, and do a final check that nothing was left behind. He carefully checked that there were no phone number impressions on notepads or such. As to Bugs … well, he would just have to take his own chances!

It was less than ten minutes later that they were in their rental car, heading back down the freeway to KL with the realization that the case had came to a rather abrupt and unplanned end. They wondered just how Martin would react to the news, hoping it wouldn't be a case of "shooting the messenger".

It was certain that Martin was not going to be happy with the news. However, as Control remarked at a later debriefing, "At least he will be able to see her in the flesh anytime he likes."

BUT WHY?

"It's not the lies they tell you; it's the lies we tell ourselves."

"But why?" is a question that I was asked even more often during my years as the Thai Private Eye than I am these days by my inquisitive daughter; and she asks that one a lot. Martin, the client from the above tale, was yet another of the many to pose that question after he learnt the results of our meeting with Ree.

This actually moves us into an area I have studied and, indeed, sometimes lecture on these days. Forgive me for breaking from the investigative reports and devoting a few pages to this topic, but it is, I think, important. I strongly believe anyone, male or female, Asian or Westerner, involved in a cross-cultural relationship, be it for business or pleasure, should have some idea of the background to the cultural and psychological differences involved. Here is what I passed onto Martin, to provide some explanation to his pained "why?".

I don't profess to be a psycho-biologist, or even *au fait* with the works of people such as Nobel Prize winner Roger Sperry, who brought to notice the differences between the brains right and left hemispheres, but I did do some minor study, and also a research paper, that looked closely at these sticky matters.

Being able to combine the wisdom of people such as Sperry and Richard Nisbett (whose book, *The Geography of Thought*, gives very good insights into the differences in thinking between Asians and Westerners) with what I had experienced myself over the many years spent in Thailand did give me perhaps a far better insight into the question of "why" than is possible for most other people without this grounding and experience.

The simple fact is that many of my years in the Kingdom were indeed spent eating, drinking and conversing with the locals, basically living in the manner of a rather normal, even average, Thai citizen. Although I initially managed hotels, these were not trendy, multinational-owned and operated resorts, and often I was the only non-Thai on the staff. My years as an investigator were spent as much in small upcountry villages, or Bangkok slums, as they were at resorts or five-star hotels. I didn't realize it at the time, but certainly during that period, my own epistemology, or way of thinking, changed accordingly.

Just to give you an example: in the "Child's Play" chapter earlier in the book, I spoke about my easy relationship with the bargirls at the After School and other nearby establishments. I regularly had cases or investigations centred around Soi Cowboy, so I knew the value of having a number of local working girls on my side whom I could casually ask for background on other girls in the area.

Actually, over the years I had had two or three queries regarding girls who had worked at the After School Bar itself. Of course, the usual, easiest mode of investigation was simply to wander in, buy plenty of drinks, and then try and spot the girl under scrutiny, or casually ask where she was. Before long, I had become something of a regular and learnt that most of the girls working there were from Surin or Buriram.

Therefore, they spoke the Cambodian dialect, Khamen, as well as Thai, and although in the class system that is quite prevalent amongst Thais, to speak Khamen labelled you as belonging to a lower class, it certainly never bothered me. This lack of regional chauvinism generally endeared me to the many working girls who hailed from that part of the country. It provided me with very good examples of how many Thai bargirls really are deeply insecure at heart, as I spoke to them in their native language and was viewed by many as a sort of big brother.

So I can understand how difficult, if not impossible, it is for someone like Martin, for example, to put himself in the shoes of a Thai women whose family could only afford to educate her until she was 12, but who, in return, expect to rely on her for survival later in life.

The interdependence of many Asians stands, of course, in

direct contrast to the independent attitude of many Westerners. For instance, in much of Southeast Asia, pensions, unemployment benefits, child allowances, sickness benefits, redundancy payments or even divorce settlements are mostly non-existent. Consequently, dependence on one's family is much greater, and perhaps a reason that the belief in or need to fulfil family obligations remains paramount. These values of duty are, in fact, instilled in daughters even more than in the sons.

One of the saddest phrases, albeit a common one, I would hear when doing the rounds of many Bangkok nightspots was "*Bua chawit*". This broadly translates to "my life is boring". Spoken in these circumstances, it becomes almost a wish to give up on their current life in the hope that the next one will be better. This type of attitude, certainly more Asian than Western, perhaps offers a key to unlocking that "why" that many puzzled Westerners keep asking.

A major miss-conception (pun intended) Westerners tend to have about Asian women (or at least, about Thais) or, indeed, often about the Asian societies as a whole, is their apparent lack of morals.

This is because so many Western visitors to Thailand are tourists who tend to spend much of their time visiting the nightlife districts. Temple visits are generally restricted to Bangkok's Wat Phra Kaew, and the Emerald Buddha, or Chiang Ma's famed Doi Suthep to take the obligatory photos. Visiting one of the

Kingdom's thousands of small rural temples at daybreak, learning what was going on there and why, would definitely show the local people in a far different light.

Probably more so than in the West, one finds that peer pressure and a strong, but seldom spoken of, class system are forces that place Thais under added stress. A family in a small rural village may feel loss of face if a neighbour has donated more to the temple than they, or if that neighbour has a new TV. Education is also a cause for pressure; to be able to send your children to university, particularly a well-known one, is indeed something to tell your neighbours about, and to show you to advantage in the "one-upmanship" stakes that Asians hold so dear.

The pressure to realise many of these aspirations again often falls primarily on the daughters in the family. The initial hope is often that your daughter will marry the son of a successful or wealthy local. More often than not, however, this plan fails and the daughter is sent to the city to find work and help support her family that way. The average Thai lady has very high moral standards. She would not consider going on a date without a chaperone, and intimacy is frowned upon, at least until an engagement has been announced. Certainly any public displays of affection are taboo. Drink, drugs, and peer pressure all tend to break these beliefs down, especially when a friend from the village, or a blood relative, has crossed that huge divide and entered the night trade. Frequently, these young women initially take that big step into the night trade as singers or karaoke hostesses. Or perhaps they will take on the status of a *mia noi* (a "minor" or show wife) that is a common occurrence in the Kingdom.

And that is the beginning of a very slippery slope. In many cases, endless requests from their families for money along with the desire to have the same accessories their friends have – such as new mobile phones, trendy clothes, and, sadly, very much needed drugs – complete the breakdown of those morals.

Once a Thai woman has crossed that boundary and entered the night trade, entered hotel rooms, she resigns herself to what she considers her fate. She will realize she no longer has any hope of marrying the wealthy Thai man her family had planned on, and also that she has failed many Buddhist teachings or beliefs, and hence has wasted or ruined this particular life. Her only salvation, she will tend to believe, is to continue to send money to help her family or siblings so that they will not have to tread the same path. By doing this, she may well become a better person, with better fortune, in the next life.

Working in the night trade, as any psychologist will tell you, also places a lot of stress on those concerned, and this is magnified when that person is young and poorly educated. Alcohol and drugs are the common and easy ways to make it through from day to day, from hotel room to hotel room As I learned from my "big-brother" conversations with many bargirls, in most cases the drink and drug-taking was just a mask to cover up tangled feelings of disgust, or to help them survive in that rather dubious occupation. With their self-esteem at a very low ebb, these Thai girls have but one avenue of regaining some pride or self-satisfaction. That is the knowledge that they are pretty and therefore admired by older, wealthier, and (supposedly) far better educated men.

From wonder bras to plastic surgery, these girls will do what they can to enhance their physical appeal, or to at least continue to draw those admiring glances from the opposite sex. In Ree's case, her self-esteem had perhaps dwindled to zero. Her brothers led good, honest, hard-working lives, but she had let her family down. She knew the husband they had earmarked for her would not even consider someone like her now.

Possibly numbed by a combination of debt and drugs, Ree felt that she had suddenly been given a chance at her 15 minutes of dubious fame. She had become someone who was admired, albeit by the wrong people for the wrong reasons. Certainly going off with Martin would have been a much wiser choice, and no doubt could have helped Ree to a far better life. However, she was at a stage where she had written this life off: "*Bua chawit.*" Thus, a combination of her fragile emotional state, of various psychological pressures, and ancient beliefs had caused her to make one bad decision after another. And that's the sad but inescapable answer to the big "why?".

I could understand why she had treated Martin like a ship in the night. She would have appreciated his interest, but probably felt she wasn't really good enough for him on a permanent basis, and also she was enjoying her bit of fame as well as the money and freedom she had at the moment. I can also see how he would struggle to understand why she didn't take the wonderful opportunity he could have offered her. Hopefully, understanding this background helped to answer Martin's and many other disillusioned Western suitors' query as to "why?".

So ends the lesson. I'm not sure if it would sail through graduate school, but without doubt, being a Thai private eye certainly provides a very good grounding in basic psychology!

THE BEST PLANNED LAYS
OF MEN AND MICE

*"The sure way to be cheated
is to think one's self more cunning than others."*
François de la Rochefoucauld

Thai Private Eye recently received an enquiry from a Hawaiian law firm that they had worked with previously. The law firm itself had been engaged by a woman who was obviously thinking along the lines of divorce proceedings, dependant on the outcome of a covert surveillance operation she had asked them to arrange during her husband's alleged upcoming "business trip" to Bangkok. (Considering the number of business trips to Thailand we at TPE hear of, Bangkok may well be the business capital of the world, although the Thai stock exchange does not seem to reflect that.)

Initially, the Hawaiian firm just supplied basic information, including the time frame and the hotel in question, and told us they would confirm the assignment with complete details, names, descriptions, et cetera in due course. The hotel mentioned was well known to us, so there was no need for a risk assessment. It was just a matter of configuring their room charges into our job estimate and confirming that we would have agents available for the period required to carry out the operation.

The firm was happy with our estimates, and forwarded further details as well as the aim of the investigation so we could formulate a full itinerary and get preparations underway. They had not yet given us the subject's name, but we did have a basic description. At that stage, the case controller put one and one together, and came up with a probable answer of two. The hotel in question, the time frame, and the physical description given all indicated it was possible that we already knew the subject.

We were in the process of completing a minor local case for a client, and, of course, didn't know his personal details; well, certainly we didn't know his current marital status. We had been hired by him to investigate his current (and no doubt, very soon to be his former) Thai girlfriend.

Our understanding was he not only doubted her integrity, but also felt the relationship had run its course. So perhaps in his own mind, he simply wanted a specific reason to end the affair, and as he stated, "move on". He had informed us he would shortly be back in Bangkok and was looking forward to getting our final report. Guess what?

This client was staying at the same hotel the Hawaiian firm had mentioned in their client's request, and at the same time. Further, he bore an uncanny resemblance to the description we had been given. Whether the gods work in mysterious ways, or you just put it down to coincidence, but for a city of over 10 million people, it's amazing how often the phrase "it's a small world" seems to crop up in and around Bangkok!

We awaited final confirmation and photographs from Hawaii before jumping to any conclusions. However, a few days later, they emailed us again, to say their client had cancelled the job. This nicely relieved us of any grappling with our conscience over matters of professional integrity or moral obligation on our part. But it was only later that it became crystal clear as to why that assignment had been cancelled.

Meanwhile, our own client had now arrived in town and booked into the hotel in question. Control still had a nagging doubt, however, so thought it wise to just plant a seed of doubt in his mind and asked about his residential location and marital status.

When told he was indeed married, and living in Hawaii, we casually suggested that perhaps one reason his wife didn't object to his frequent trips to the Land of Smiles was just possibly because she was trying to catch him out with another woman. After all, he was a fairly wealthy man, and it could prove very costly to him if such was the case.

At a meeting to hand over our final reports and DVDs which confirmed that his current girlfriend, like so many of her ilk, was seriously into drugs and gambling, it was suggested he make use of one of our close-protection personnel during his stay. Apart from possibly being himself checked on by his wife, we were sure that when his current girlfriend got her marching orders from the up-market apartment he had rented for her and the obligatory friends or hangers-on that Thai women with wealthy boyfriends tend to acquire, she would not be very happy and things might well turn nasty.

As he was wealthy and had a lot to lose, especially on the possible divorce issue, it seemed a prudent move. However, he was so self-confident, indeed arrogant, that he merely passed it off as our being paranoid and attempting to get further work off him. He said that his wife was simply not clever enough to employ anyone to check up on him, as he had done with his girlfriend. He also added he would simply give the current Thai girl some money to "go away".

There was little we could do then, except shake our heads and wonder how someone so adept in the commercial world could be so ignorant of the female world, especially regarding Thai women involved in the night trade. (Which is where, of course, he had found the girlfriend.) He told our representative that he had everything under control, and not to waste his breath using what he termed "scare tactics" on him.

He was, however, still our client, so our man again reminded him to be alert for any possible investigation organized by his wife, and to at least perhaps change hotels. It was further suggested he should certainly keep his whereabouts concealed from the apparently soon-to-be former Thai girlfriend when he ended that relationship. Advice, I should add, that he just waved away in the same cocky manner he believed he would be able to dismiss the girlfriend with.

We do pride ourselves in putting our client's needs and well-being first, and most are generally thankful for any additional help or advice we offer. In this case, as we learnt a little later on, another very common Thai phrase was certainly applicable: "*Som nom nar*". (This is a Thai phrase, very often heard and meaning something like "serves you right" or "you got what you deserved.")

Our Bangkok patch being the surprisingly small world it is, we soon got word back that the Thai girlfriend had indeed been most unhappy about being shown the red card! As we had predicted, the now ex-girlfriend had turned to stalking our client, even physically attacking him one night, which resulted in his requiring a trip to hospital to get stitched up. She repeatedly came to his hotel, where he had remained despite our warning, and generally abused him at every opportunity – an ongoing tirade that apparently continues against the man to this very day, whenever she finds he's back in Bangkok.

Thai women certainly do tend to have "stickability". No matter what you say or do, it is rare for any Thai you have befriended in the past to just walk away when asked – especially one you have made substantial monetary contributions to. Your phone number and email address will never get deleted, and it seems you are always kept in mind. Whether it's that they believe there is some vague chance of a further windfall at some stage, or because they wish to remember your details so that they can continue to ask the gods to inflict grief or bad luck upon you, I'm not quite sure!

Our arrogant client obviously did not have the most memorable sojourn in the Land of Smiles on that particular occasion. However, his worst troubles were yet to begin.

On his return to Hawaii, neither his wife nor their grown-up son and daughter were at the airport to meet him, which was rather unusual. He called his palatial home a number of times, but, again strangely, there was no answer. He had to resort to hailing a taxi to complete his journey home. There he was met by his siblings and some other relatives, standing outside the family mansion and not apparently all that pleased to see him.

Apparently, that's when things really started plunging downhill for this fellow! He was prevented from entering his own home, as the locks had all been changed. His wife was nowhere to be seen, his own family had taken sides against him. He was now in total confusion – until he was actually handed a photo album featuring shots of him with various Thai girls ... taking them to his hotel room at night, coming out with them in the morning, sometimes with more than one. All were nicely chronicled with dates, times, even incidents of bargirls he knew, or in confrontations with his ex-Thai girlfriend. Hotel receipts for multiple breakfasts, mini-bar and laundry receipts were all included – even some of the Thai girls' full names and dates of birth that would have been obtained from their ID cards, held for security purposes by the hotel at reception during their brief stays. A full report of the attack on him by the aggrieved ex-girlfriend and his subsequent hospital treatment was also included. Not our work, but we had to admit, it was a job well done ... and a job which could not have come cheaply!

His clothes and personal belongings were all in a trailer hooked up to his 4WD, parked in the drive and ready to go. Like the investigators, the locksmith, and everything else his antagonists had hired, it had been paid for with his money. His expensive sports car was, however, locked away in the multi-garage of his home. That was the last straw, so, rather deflated, he could do little but retreat to a local hotel for a few days to reassess his situation.

All this information came to us in dribs and drabs over the following few months, both from the would-be Hawaii 5-O star himself and from various locals and bargirls who, one way or another, had come into contact with him.

It transpired that although his wife was indeed quiet, unassuming, and no doubt prepared to overlook his indiscretions in view of the luxurious lifestyle she enjoyed, his son and daughter were not so forgiving, and it was they who had initiated the investigation.

Computer savvy, they had some time back installed a key logger on their father's PC, and so had cracked his passwords. From there, reading through his emails, his sordid Thai history became very clear. Although claiming they were mostly upset by the humiliation their mother was facing, it was more likely the fact they could foresee their vast future inheritance being shared by a string of Thai bargirls that served as the catalyst for their strong reaction. Just to rub some premium salt into the wound, they had actually financed what had become a very expensive investigation with a spare credit card he had left with his wife "for emergencies".

The cost of the investigation was so high due to the fact that they had opted to bring in a Singaporean PI firm. This was necessary after the lawyers had originally advised the man's family that Thai Private Eye could handle the investigation. From having read his emails, the son and daughter were well aware that their father had, in fact, employed us himself, so they evidently made a frantic call to the lawyers and told them not to divulge any further facts to us. They then found a company not based in Thailand to carry out the investigation. As the bill was being footed by his credit card, the expense was irrelevant. Consequently, the Singapore firm put three teams on the assignment, conducting 24-hour surveillance; thus, the very thorough and professional job.

It was not too long before the man himself was back in Bangkok and, all too predictably, soon found yet another Thai girl he was besotted with and planned to marry. We thought perhaps he had learnt a little, as he called us to arrange a basic background check on any past husbands or children, or related obstacles. We had just begun the investigation when he called again, advising us to cancel any further work, as he now knew not only would she not lie to him, she was, in fact, "the one". The requested dowry had been paid, and the village wedding planned for the following week.

(Thai weddings are commonly held in upcountry villages, usually in the presence of monks, and involve a number of traditional rites. All parties are then happy that the marriage is official, although this is not, in fact, the case until that marriage is registered at the local municipal office or police station. This, however, is not always done, making the confirmation of whether a Thai person has actually been married previously not always as straightforward as our clients might expect.)

Just what the current state of play is in this relationship, is anyone's guess. However, this Hawaiian was one client who very much fit the bill of the male tourist who arrives in Asia with a lot of money and is looking for a girl with some experience. By the time most of these men leave, the girls will have the money, and they will have the experience!

Shortly thereafterwards, we did, however, meet with a client who wisely took Thai Private Eye's suggestions very seriously. This astute gentleman hailed from the Land of the Rising Sun.

Japan certainly does more than its fair share to boost the Thai economy. Over the years they have provided more aid and assistance than all other countries combined. While Thai law restricts foreign ownership in most instances, there are, of course, always loopholes, and many Thai companies owe their financial position and success to Japanese backing and management.

Consequently, there are many well-paid Japanese executives based in Bangkok, of which Mr Tobe was one. Their affluence is also not lost on some Thai women keen to increase the family fortunes. Those who bother to learn some of the Japanese language, and in particular the karaoke songs, can make four or five times more working in Soi Taniya than their sisters working in the adjacent Patpong bars. While many Thai girls are happy to have a Western sponsor who may give them a gold bracelet and forward around US$500 per month, those who can get themselves a Japanese executive as a sponsor may well receive US$2000 plus per month, more than most entire Thai families earn per year. In addition, they often receive a car to go with the gold bracelet, along with the obligatory up-market apartment.

(Soi Taniya, by the way, is a small lane adjacent to the more well-known red light area of Bangkok known as Patpong. The majority of bars in this lane have a "karaoke" flavour and are restricted to Japanese patrons only. Cost of services, drinks and ladies is considerably higher – whether performance justifies that, we cannot say, but certainly some of the more attractive and better educated Thai girls involved in the entertainment industry are to be found at this location.)

Tobe had gone past the sponsorship stage and had married his Thai girlfriend. The demanded dowry, or *sin sot* as it's known, had been large and been paid, and the couple now lived in a very plush apartment. His wife had ample spending money and time to visit friends or go shopping while Tobe was at work, or on the weekends when he indulged in his other favoured pastime: playing golf.

Lately, however, a few little inconsistencies and unexplained happenings were bugging him just enough to have him come and have a chat with our team. These little annoyances included things such as secretive text messages or the home phone occasionally going unanswered when the wife should have been at home. Nothing much, but put together, something he felt needed to be looked into. (Strangely enough, in all my years as a PI, there was rarely an occasion when a client who had doubts or misgivings about someone was found to be wrong!) Various options were discussed, and our hi-tech expert's idea to go with a GPS tracking device installed in the wife's vehicle was the one that most appealed to Tobe, so plans were made to run an operation based around one of those very handy devices.

As there was an upcoming regional conference in Singapore that Tobe would be attending, so the surveillance was planned to coincide with that. He left his company vehicle at work on the Friday and told his wife he would be taking a taxi to the airport on Monday morning. Meanwhile, he would use her car on Saturday morning to meet up with his usual foursome out at the very pleasant Windsor Park golf course. That, then, was the first step in getting us the vehicle and giving our experts the time required to covertly install the GPS device.

Attention to detail is, of course, paramount in our trade, so to begin with, photos were taken of the car's interior to make sure all her personal items went back in the correct place. The floor mats were carefully lifted out, making sure all relevant dirt and rubbish remained in place and got put back on completion of the installation. Having the car go for a "grooming" is often much easier, but as Tobe had told us, he had never washed his wife's car, so sending it for a valet cleaning in this instance would probably have aroused her counter-suspicions.

Monday morning and all was in readiness. Tobe called us when he was in the taxi heading to the airport. His wife had said she would probably go upcountry to visit her parents for a few days, so she might not be able to contact him, as there was no mobile coverage in that particular remote area. Tobe had assured her that was fine and told her he would be back home

Thursday evening.

The wife's movements were then easily monitored or tracked in real time on our computers, and once she was out and about, it was evident she was not heading towards her parents' home in Chantaburi. The car was instead tracked to a medium-class block of apartments in the Ratchada district, so she may well have just gone to visit friends.

Little action was noted until later in the evening, when the vehicle moved a few kilometres down the road to Rhamkamheng Soi 39 and into the car park at the up-market restaurant and nightclub called The Glass Home. Soon a couple of our agents were on the scene and wandered into the establishment known as a hang-out for trendy young Thais, many of whom were supposedly studying at the nearby university. It took them a little while to locate Tobe's wife, but eventually they found her at a small table, apparently gazing deeply into the eyes of her dinner date, a *farang*.

The guy in question was, however, markedly different to her husband. Whereas Tobe was in his fifties, bespectacled, balding and would have looked rather out of place in such surroundings, the man with our client's wife certainly did not. This fellow was about her age, late twenties, fit and good-looking. The agents had trouble gauging his nationality, as he spoke fluent Thai.

Our agents in this case could hardly have been described as being in the young-and-hip swinging set either, so after getting a couple of discreet photos, they retreated to the car park and waited to see what developed. Whether the man was just a casual acquaintance or something rather more than that would, they hoped, soon be revealed.

A few hours later, some vehicle movement was noted, and not surprisingly, the car went back to the Ratchada apartments. A number of agents were nearby, and just in case the two who had tracked Tobe's wife in the nightclub were recognized, it was another pair of our Thai agents who just happened to wander through the apartment doors the same time as did the happy couple. Said happy couple had obviously had a pleasant, alcohol-soaked evening on Tobe's hard-earned yen. Apart from some shopping trips, the vehicle remained at the apartments for most of the week while Tobe was in Singapore.

One of our female Thai agents, feigning interest in the *farang*, approached the rather plain-looking apartment receptionist to seek more information about the hunk. This receptionist obviously fancied the playboy herself (although to no avail evidently) and was able to confirm that Mr Martin was, in fact, an Australian teacher, and that his rich girlfriend often visited him.

Tobe returned home towards the end of the week and used the same golfing excuse to return the vehicle to us, to pick up our reports, and to also let us retrieve the GPS. That latter is a handy piece of equipment which in a city like Bangkok can be an invaluable tool in vehicle tracking. Similar apparatuses we have tried, such as magnetic slap and track sticks, we found both expensive and unreliable in comparison to the GPS.

Tobe was, of course, disappointed in his wife's actions. As he pointed out, after six or seven years of marriage, he could have understood it, but after only six or seven months, it was a bit hard to take. Nonetheless, he was very pragmatic and had also taken the precaution of having her sign a pre-nuptial agreement; he wasn't a company CEO for nothing!

We had learnt her affair with Martin had been going on for some time. In fact, she had met him when she went for some English lessons prior to learning Japanese. She was somewhat pragmatic herself, in that she put marriage to a wealthy Japanese man ahead of having fun with someone closer to her own age. However, once financially secure (or so she thought), she had again linked up with the guy she herself was infatuated with. We did manage to get into a conversation with a friend of Martin's at his local bar and learnt that the Lothario teacher was himself enamoured with a new young student, parallel to his being regularly wined and dined by the wife of a wealthy Japanese.

What did I say about *wen gum*, the Thai equivalent of "Do unto others"? Tobe went ahead and completed divorce proceedings immediately, slightly consoled to learn his ex would not become the respected partner of an esteemed teacher, as she imagined. He was also grateful to us, and the use of a GPS, for bringing his wife's indiscretions to light so quickly.

WHAM, SCAM, THANK YOU MA'AM

*"A fool and his money are soon parted.
And the older the fool, the sooner the parting."*
Time-tested proverb

It had not been a particularly good month for the team at Thai Private Eye. Certainly in a business such as ours, things do not always go to plan or run smoothly. We had literally just run full smack into the consequences of taking on a job where the client had not passed on all relevant information to us, and even worse, was not in full possession of all the facts himself.

The Singaporean had seen his Thai girlfriend disappear a few months earlier and had just about exhausted all avenues of finding or contacting her himself, when she was seen by a friend of his. Adding to the drama, she was seen in a department store maternity shop and it was very obvious she was shopping for herself. Desperate not only to contact her, but to get her back to Singapore, where he assumed maternity hospitals would provide better care for their soon-to-be-born child, he enlisted our help. Oh, he somehow forgot to tell us that she had deliberately avoided his own efforts to contact her recently, and, oh yes, he also failed to inform us that her previous boyfriend was a very experienced Thai kick boxer! Little details like that do help our investigations.

Add to this the facts (that we were not aware of until too late) that the kick boxer knew about Mr Singapore's efforts to contact the girl and had told him to keep clear or else and that, rather than being an "ex" boyfriend, it was he who was the child's actual father. You can get some idea of the disaster our agents sailed into. Suffice it to say, we had some rather badly beaten agents to care for and were not at all happy with Mr Singapore. Consequently, we now are extremely careful in accepting any cases that we believe we have not been fully briefed on.

The job request we received a few days later from an elderly European, however, did seem relatively straightforward and perhaps offered us a chance to give our agents a safe and injury-free assignment. Of course, just what the connection was between an elderly, quiet, reserved, and extremely wealthy Belgian gentleman and a "wanna-be-rich" middle-aged Macau expat playboy was something that would only be revealed in the fullness of time.

Edmond was wealthy; not just rich, he was obscenely rich. The owner of a successful Brussels-based electronics company, he was now semi-retired, and one of his hobbies had been surfing the Net, and in particular, some Asian dating sites. It was through this dubious medium that he had come across the vivacious Miss Angelina.

(How dubious a medium, you ask. The case of the Internet scammer, detailed in my *Confessions of a Bangkok Private Eye* gives an in-depth look at how some people online differ greatly from their site profile – not only in looks, but often in age and gender as well!)

An accurate description of Angelina would run something along these lines: age 31, born in Bangkok; mother, Thai, father, allegedly American; occupation, actress /gold-digger. She could also lay claim to the very dangerous attributes of brains, beauty, patience, and, of course, greed. Again, just like Edmond, it was sometime into the investigation before we were fully aware of all these facts.

Having jetted out to Bangkok to meet the lovely Angelina, and finding that in this case, rather surprisingly to us, that she did indeed exist and in the flesh was actually fairly much like her stunning online profile, Edmond had then spent the next two years showering her with gifts, gold, money, and trips all around Europe and Asia. He also had financially supported her supposed acting career and even thrown in the obligatory car for her and a new home for Momma. They were – well, better make that Edmond was – in love. She had met his friends and family, including his daughters, who were about her own age, and by that point, Edmond was sure she was perfect wife material.

It's at that time that our patient gold-digger goes for the jugular and tells Edmond to forward funds for their future dream mansion. And believe me, even in Thailand, dream mansions overlooking the Andaman Sea do not come cheap.

The exceptionally large transfer of funds was made, and Edmond was happy to do so as they were going into a joint account for the home that he believed would be held jointly in their names. Well, dear reader, hazard a guess as to what happens next? Amazing, you must be psychic!

It wasn't long before both the funds and the lovely Angelina seemingly disappeared into oblivion. It was at this stage that Edmond contacted us, not worried about his missing money, but to try and ascertain what had happened to his beloved. He feared she may have been in an accident, or perhaps robbed and beaten by the estate agent! As he relayed the whole story to us, he did mention the odd time when Angelina had gone missing in the past for a week or two. Allegedly, she was on photo shoots in remote locations. There was also the occasional phone call late at night, or taken out of his hearing, that he assured us were work-related, and it became obvious that this was a carefully planned and well-executed scam on her part. That is, obvious to us anyway!

Edmond, of course, was still not convinced Angelina would have set him up in such a way, so as the "customer is always right", we agreed with him and treated this as a missing persons case, rather than a huge missing money scam on a rich old gentleman by a smart, attractive girl!

We went through the motions of checking local hospitals, with the suspected negative result, then had a police contact check files to see if any arrest or felony had been reported involving her; again, nothing was found. That, of course, left another department and other contacts to chat with, where we finally met with some success. The lady in question had indeed departed the Kingdom, just a few days after Edmond's substantial transfer had been completed, and taken the night flight direct to Macau. According to our information (and yes, we have to keep some secrets as to how we obtain all our material), she was staying at the famed Lisboa Hotel.

Edmond was then called and updated. As the investigation was still ongoing, and mindful of the problems our agents had only recently encountered, he was informed that she was in Macau, but we didn't at that stage pass on the name of the hotel we believed she was staying at. Edmond would undoubtedly have called the hotel, or probably flown out in a private jet, and could have compromised the case. We simply asked if he wanted us to continue and perhaps gather some photographic evidence. Not in a great frame of mind to begin with, he understandably was not too pleased with our findings. At first, he accused us of lying about locating her. We countered by offering to happily continue the investigation and pledged we would either get hard evidence for him within 48 hours or refund his retainer.

A now somewhat subdued client agreed that we should continue, and a further payment for expenses was immediately forwarded to us from Brussels. We had two agents heading for Macau later that evening. Although a large and bustling hotel, the Lisboa has only one major breakfast or 24-hour coffee shop. It was there the following morning that our alert team was well-positioned to scope out the scene. For a time, they just sat, amused by the range of Chinese and Russian prostitutes parading past, trying to snare clients on their way to the downstairs casino, or perhaps to catch one of the few winners on his way out. Then one member of the team spotted Angelina with some guy whom we soon learnt was Shane, an Australian professional gambler. Not so actively involved in casino games of chance, he apparently did considerably better at the Macau and Hong Kong racetracks than most.

Looking like a honeymoon couple, it was quite obvious Shane and Angelina were not in some platonic relationship. We could only surmise that in the upstairs suite where they spent most of their time, the form Shane was studying closely was not just that of thoroughbreds. Mind you, one has to concede that in the world of gold-diggers and scam artists, Angelina was something of a champion. Our agents did not have to spend long in the hotel to get a number of pictures of an apparently very loving couple. For his part, Shane was much closer to Angelina's age, and a late-night drinking and dancing session at the nearby Fortuna nightclub provided more evidence of them both having a good time, in a manner that was well past Edmond's current physical capabilities.

Our agents emailed a number of pics back to the Bangkok office, one showing that day's *China Post* very prominently, and these were, in turn, forwarded on to Edmond.

Our information was that Angelina would not be returning to Bangkok for some time, wise girl that she was. However, Edmond advised us that he was on his way to the Kingdom and asked whether we could meet him at the airport, so we could go through all the details and, in his words, "help sort this out". It's not our normal procedure to meet clients this way, but Edmond had spent a fair amount of money with us to date.

Moreover, we did have some concerns for his safety, especially as he had made mention to us that Angelina had recently told him she had some powerful connections in the Thai police force. This was more likely a calculated bluff on her part to keep him from trying to track her down after she had worked her scam. But in view of the recent events and confrontations our agents had faced, we were not going to take any chances. She would know that Edmond had the funds to mount a very serious hunt for her, and with the cash she now had at her disposal, getting someone to protect her, or harm him, would likewise not be too difficult.

We met the rather gaunt, sombre Edmond as arranged, and accompanied him to the Hyatt. Once he had checked in, we adjourned to his suite and went over all details we had gathered to date. He still did not totally accept that he had been taken for a first-class ride; he felt there were unknown pressures or circumstances that had forced Angelina to act the way she did. However, our agent's reports from Macau and accompanying photographs proved that she was under no duress whilst with her Australian roommate, and they were quite obviously comfortable together. It was then that we pointed to those times she was out of contact, took secretive phone calls, or made reference to various events or alleged photo shoots, some that we had since confirmed never took place. Bit by bit, Edmond then recalled numerous other questionable happenings during the relationship.

By the time we left him, he was resigned to the fact that perhaps we were right, and his mood of concern and worry was about due to be replaced by anger and good old lust for revenge! He called us the next morning. (No doubt it had been a restless night for the man from Brussels.) He wanted us to track her down with a team of our special bodyguards on hand. The cost, he repeatedly informed us, was no object. We pointed out that she would more than likely have bodyguards herself, and that as foreigners, even with our contacts, a confrontation at the airport, or anywhere in Thailand for that matter, was something we were never going to win. We also advised him that as far as we were aware, she had moved from Macau to Hong Kong, and had no bookings to return anytime soon to the Land of Smiles.

In the end, Edmond agreed to leave the matter with us. We

would keep the case open and advise him if and when we learnt of her whereabouts. But for the time being, that was as far as we would go. When we called back to his suite later that night, he had already checked out, obviously not in any mood to bother about making further acquaintances with Thai women.

I know, it's becoming repetitive, but it's a fact: Bangkok is a very small place. Either that, or the gods there enjoy playing the fate and coincidence cards. About a week after Edmond's departure, we received an email from Hong Kong. A certain Australian gentleman was asking about our services, with an eye to running a background check on a young Thai lady who just happened to go by the name of Angelina!

Edmond was, to all intents and purposes, still our client, and although we struggled with the coincidence of it all, and in fact wondered at first if it was some kind of set up instigated by the Brussels gentleman himself, we ran our own checks and found we were indeed dealing with a now Hong Kong-based, "ow-yah-goin-mate" Aussie.

Cautiously asking for a little more detail as to the type of information he was after, we were told it was basically a financial and credibility check. The woman in question had shown him a suitcase containing "a helluva lot of cash" and was asking him to match it as an investment based around the production of a new Thai movie. The money was to be deposited in a joint account, and yes, that account would be in a Thai bank. Obviously, our little scammer was out to double her holdings. I spent a day or two trying to figure out how we could possibly scam the scammer, but just ended up with a headache.

In the end, I went with the easiest option, and accepted a nice little *gratis* payment from both Edmond and Shane. What for, you may ask? Simple: introducing them to each other.

A VIEW FROM THE OTHER SIDE

"You know you're in love when you no longer want your girlfriend (or boyfriend) hanging out at the place where you picked her/him up."
Thai Private Eye maxim

There are a number of places in Southeast Asia which have the distinction of being something of a haven for those with other than heterosexual tendencies. Thailand is clearly one. I guess I had a fair insight into the Thai perspective on this, and could work out some of the whys and wherefores behind this phenomenon.

You must consider that it is common for the Thai father or husband to be either away working in the city, or perhaps to have simply "fled the scene". Add to this the fact that a young boy or brother is particularly revered in Thai society, to the point where they are often spoilt and constantly hugged and cuddled by friends and family, particularly mothers or sisters, and the foundations for encouraging somewhat effeminate behaviour later in life are perhaps laid back there in the home.

I found in my travels that lesbianism was quite common amongst young girls working in bars and clubs. More often than not, this had stemmed from too many "broken hearts" caused by the opposite sex, or else fulfilling a need to have someone close who understood their particular wants, needs, and fears, something that an older, foreign beau could not. Unlike Westerners, who often value some time alone, many Thais tend to have a fear of being on their own, particularly at night!

Thais are also particularly prone to "wearing their hearts on their sleeve" and emotionally seem to mirror the ups and downs of the local daily soap operas, to which many are addicted. Sure, there are those who have become hardened, almost mechanical, over the years. But for many, their relationships tend to resemble walking on eggshells rather than steady and stable affairs. Drama Queen is a term that, for better or worse, can be applied to many Thai ladies of the night. It is quite common to spot a few "slash" marks on a pretty young girl's wrists, and on a few occasions, even I had the dubious honour of having such a mark pointed out and told "this one because of you!" Of course, in true Thai style, the slashes are rarely as deep as the ones I give myself shaving, but you get the point.

There are also many instances in the Bangkok night scene of heterosexuals changing their outlook or preference, simply for the better monetary opportunities it may offer. It was not uncommon, therefore, for Thai Private Eye to be contacted to look into certain cases or relationships that were of a homosexual nature. Of course, there were also times, such as in the intriguing "Case of the Reluctant Virgin" detailed in my earlier book, *Confessions of a Bangkok Private Eye*, where the client was unknowingly in such a relationship!

In the following case, however, it was clear that everyone knew very well just what was going on, at least from a sexual point of view. It did also, for better or worse, provide the agent assigned the case quite an insight (dare I say even more than he wanted) into the goings on in some of the city's gay bars. This story lets you share some of what he learnt there.

First, let me say that I, and indeed all those at Thai Private Eye, are fairly broadminded, and in no way judgmental about anyone's sexuality or sexual preferences. I apologize if I offend anyone with this case or the rather explicit details with which our assigned agent was confronted at times. But hey, this book is based on actual cases as they happened, so you need to know the facts! We do certainly find ourselves in all types of situations, and I can only repeat, after a good many years in the trade, that nothing surprises me these days.

We received an email asking us for advice and help in a case involving a man and his 20-year-old Thai male lover. According to the client, they had met in a male go-go bar in the Patpong Soi

4 area of Bangkok, a well-known haven for the gay fraternity.

In the same manner as often happens to Western male tourists meeting girls working in the bars and clubs on the adjacent *sois* or lanes around Patpong, these two soon became more seriously involved, to the extent that the Thai lad had convinced our client it would be a great idea to open a beauty salon in Bangkok that he would manage for him. This seemed like a sound idea, as it would get the young Adonis away from the clutches of the bar's many customers and hopefully allow him to earn a more legitimate salary.

Being a successful businessman himself, our client was not totally naive, and he wanted to get some confirmation that his investment, which would possibly total quite a few thousand of Uncle Sam's dollars, was not going to be wasted.

The initial part of the investigation therefore was to ascertain that the Thai toy boy was at least carrying out his part of the bargain. This meant to cease working in the gay bar scene and to attend a beautician school to acquire the necessary knowledge and certificates. I had carried out many similar requests for clients checking on Thai girls allegedly intent on heading down a similar straight and narrow path and, in most instances, ended up having to report that the call of the bar was generally more powerful than the call of the beautician school. I wondered if things were any different as far as Thai males were concerned. I had previously carried out a few minor investigations for Western men checking out Thai males, but in most of those cases, they either concealed the target's background or their own particular reason of interest.

We had previously not had the need or urge to take a closer look at Bangkok's gay club community. However, as the city had the perhaps dubious claim to being the sex capital of the world, we were in no doubt it would be full-on, with all tastes well catered for. Indeed, even just wandering around the Patpong night markets, one is continuously tapped on the shoulder and asked, "You want lady?" If, for whatever reason, you happen to answer "No, thanks", you can be sure of an immediate follow-up question: "You want boy?"

Allowing for the flocks of customers such places undoubtedly draw, not to mention the stigma of various diseases associated even more with homosexuals, it was not surprising then that as our client was a very caring guy, he wanted to see his new love get out of his current environment ASAP. To quote again a well-known TPE maxim, "You know you're in love when you don't want your girl (or boyfriend) hanging around in the place you met her or him!"

Case accepted, we then had our own internal problem to deal with. Although we have what we consider a wide range of agents, of different races, both full-time and casual, as far as we are aware, none of them happened to be both Westerners and gay. Or Asian and gay, for that matter. It's no problem at all finding an agent willing to sit in a normal go-go bar and try and see if a particular girl is working or "available". However, in this case, we needed someone to spend perhaps a fair amount of time in the city's gay bars, and what's more, appear as though he were totally enjoying the experience!

We are very particular about those we employ, and also make sure that they are well trained in our methods and procedures, so taking a chance on a casual outsider with bona fide gay credentials was not something we would consider. Instead, we put out a sort of call for volunteers amongst those agents we had who at least looked as though they might fit the gay mode.

It took some talking, along with an offer of a bonus, to convince one of our younger agents to take on the job. His main concern was not that he'd be thought of as having homosexual tendencies, which he certainly did not, but that he would, in fact, be found out when in a gay bar or club as not being a … bona fide "member of the fraternity" is perhaps the phrase to use. He was afraid that if he were somehow "outed", he might suffer a whipping or some other unwanted form of beating, bondage or domination! We assured him we would have ample back-up stationed in the immediate area in case this problem ever looked like it might materialize, and also made a point of swearing the client to secrecy regarding the investigation. Any hint to his new partner that he may be checked up on, would, of course, have the toy boy even more on the alert for someone such as our agent. The client was duly reminded that it was imperative he act as normal as possible while the investigation was being conducted on his boyfriend, which he completely understood and vowed to do.

The first phase of the investigation was simply to visit the club and see if the subject was still working there and perhaps even try to determine if he was still plying his trade. He may have been sitting at home being honest and faithful, but if the men working in Bangkok's entertainment scene were anything like the girls, it was most unlikely, we figured, that he was in any haste to be chaste.

I had arranged for a contact of mine, who was a *katooey*, or transvestite, to spend a few hours with our selected agent (who was now known as Jay Jay), perhaps take him shopping, and answer any basic questions he might have. Cross-dressing "Annie" was something of a classic. When a friend had first introduced him/her to me in the dimness of the trendy Spasso nightclub one evening, it hadn't even dawned on me that "she" was not the attractive, well-groomed, articulate Thai women she seemed to be – and it certainly hadn't dawned on this other friend!

I did overhear a whisper or two in Thai that first raised my doubts, so out of curiousity I had taken the opportunity to perform my "arm test" on Annie later that evening. In the arm test, you ask the person being tested to thrust an arm out straight. When a male holds his arm out straight from the shoulder, in the manner of throwing a "straight left", it will indeed form an almost straight line. With a female performing the same act, the arm will actually bend back slightly beyond the 360° angle at the elbow joint.

Afterwards, I told Annie that "she" was the best-looking "lady-boy" I had ever seen, adding in confidence that I would keep her gender to myself. When asked what I did for a living, I gave "her" my usual line, that I helped people with visa or immigration problems. This, of course, perked up the interest of Thai girls who tended to mix with foreigners, as most had offers or queries about overseas travel. After that, I did have the odd call for advice from Annie on such matters, and there were also occasions, such as the present one, when I was able to call on "her" for some ideas.

Accordingly, Jay Jay was as well-briefed and prepared as we could manage, and so the following evening, with two of our Thai martial arts experts sitting at a nearby food stall sharing some noodles, he somewhat gingerly dipped his toe into the waters of the Patpong gay bar scene. Almost identical to the bars a *soi* or two further down Silom Road, a central catwalk with chrome poles was the focal point of this particular establishment. The catwalk itself was surrounded by some comfortable swivel chairs for those who wanted to be close up, whilst sofas and discreet booths were placed a little further back.

Jay Jay opted for a sofa, ordered a drink, and in due course was approached by a muscular young Thai guy wearing nothing other than tight white boxer shorts and baby oil. The bulge inside the shorts left little to the imagination as to what was on offer! The guy asked if he could join our intrepid agent for a drink, an offer Jay Jay politely refused. He didn't want to get chatty with anyone if it could be helped, except possibly the subject of the investigation.

The Village People and the Backstreet Boys pumped out a stream of foot-tapping music as groups of around a dozen young guys at a time took to the catwalk and gyrated around the poles, wearing only posing pouches. They spent twenty or thirty minutes showing off their moves and trying to catch the eye of any potential drink buyer or customer before being replaced by another fresh set of young Asian Adonises.

Jay Jay struggled through a couple of excruciating hours, having to buy an occasional drink and chat with various admirers, but as far as he was aware, there was no sign of the subject. Once certain he had seen all the guys in the club who took to the catwalk that evening, he bade his newfound friends farewell, and beat a hasty retreat. It was possible our client's lad had indeed retired from the club scene. Then again, perhaps he was just taking a night off, or even holidaying with yet another sponsor. For now, however, there was no sighting, so Jay Jay was happy to get outside, back to the type of bar and surroundings he was more comfortable with, and fill his interested co-workers in on the intricate details of the action inside a gay bar.

The apparent highlight of the evening, or so Jay Jay informed us, was the floor show: several naked young men descending a flight of multi-coloured stairs with nothing but an "Egyptian cock ring" around the base of their very erect penises! Although to me that accessory sounded like something to be found around the leg of a bird at a cock fight, our new expert on such matters, agent Jay Jay, explained that the dancers taking part in the floor show used the device to prolong their erections, as the rubber Egyptian ring stopped the flow of blood once the penis was erect. It was obvious that the guys placed the rings on first, then they all must have stimulated each other together in order to get an erection, so that they all came down the stairs together; something like synchronized swimming Jay Jay reckoned!

He said it made him feel uncomfortable, so he reckoned it was even more so for those taking part, who had proceeded to present their manhood to the first row of male onlookers for closer inspection. This, of course, was well received by the customers, except for Jay Jay, who supposedly tried not to look too interested! Of course, customers could then sort of hand pick which dancer they would like to have join them for a drink – or discuss some extracurricular activities with.

The show, however, was certainly not yet over. It continued with naked men being suspended from the ceiling by chains and/or strapped into a sort of gynaecologist's chair while others simulated (he hoped) having anal and oral sex with them on stage. As in Bangkok's Girlie bars, all the boys had numbers so you could order the one of your choice; perhaps in a combination deal with a cocktail, I suggested!

These numbers, which the dancers retained for their whole career at that establishment, helped customers recall a particular performer and also proved very handy for private eyes trying to confirm if a subject was still working at a venue. The fact that there was no appearance by Number 18 had convinced Jay Jay that the young man being checked up on was not working that night – at least, not in that particular club.

We suggested to Jay Jay that he should perhaps return one more time, but he made it clear he saw that as above and beyond the bounds of duty, then reminded us of a comment made when we had first taken him on board: "We won't ask you to do anything we wouldn't do ourselves." That then effectively ended Phase One, so we moved onto the next stage of the investigation.

This began with a basic surveillance of the beautician training academy in Siam Square, and we were soon able to verify that the subject was, in fact, attending the course daily, so at least he was keeping his word as far as that part of the agreement was concerned. Whether he had completely severed his links with the excitement of the gay club and sex scene was another question altogether. After some discussion with our client, we decided to conduct a covert surveillance of the lad's apartment to wrap up our investigation.

After three days of constant surveillance, tracking the subject when we could, it was not at all surprising to us to discover he was indeed working elsewhere. He had been clever enough to assume that possibly his newfound sponsor would ask some acquaintances to call by the original club just to see if Number 18 was still strutting his stuff. He had obviously not counted on this sponsor hiring a team of professionals to do the job! From the outside, his new place of work seemed innocuous enough. However, knowing Thailand as we do, we knew better than to always take things at face value.

At first glance, the establishment seemed to be little more than a fitness and bodybuilding club. However, when two of our agents approached the entrance, one casually holding a video camera and the other asking a few questions, they were very quickly turned away. Obviously, that only fuelled our interest in the club, so we switched to a different approach. Thanks to open source information and the world of the Net, we soon found the club's small website and a number to call for information. There we discovered that the club had a wide range of offerings for the discerning male wanting some discreet and exotic fitness-oriented activities, including a large number of vitamins and various substances – all guaranteed to enlarge, prolong, improve, and enhance the activities of the pertinent body parts.

A somewhat reluctant Jay Jay was then called in again to resume his role. A call was made to the club, mention was made of a "friend's" very high recommendation, and Jay Jay's name was noted. He was told to report to the club that evening and give his name to the doorman, who would be happy to allow him entry as a non-member for a mere US$20.

Using another of our agents, one who doubled as a taxi driver and was able to park nearby, Jay Jay was delivered to the club which was situated across the Chao Phraya River in the Pin Gow district, not too far from the well-known Wat Arun, the temple of dawn. But as Jay Jay was soon to learn, what the customers at this club were watching rise, certainly wasn't the sun.

The club's theme was bodybuilding exercises on a stage with simulated sex acts. Along with the various steroids and other bodybuilding drugs available, Jay Jay was left in no doubt as to how fit and strong many of the performers were. He was soon able to identify the subject, who was not yet as muscled up as many of his colleagues, but who was definitely up to par on the simulated sex moves! Jay Jay noted that some clients disappeared upstairs with staff, so there obviously were "short-time" rooms available for those who couldn't wait to test some of the products, or personnel, on offer. Although he certainly was not going to make an offer to test the sexual prowess of our client's boyfriend, he was in no doubt as to his availability.

Apart from watching the ongoing show, Jay Jay politely spurned all offers of membership deals and the array of both boys and stimulants made to him before making his exit as soon as possible.

The staff appeared rather cautious, and Jay Jay's main fear was that somehow his cover would be blown. No doubt what regularly happens when we are out and about is that there are those working in the venues other than our particular client's interests, who are likewise doing so against a sponsor's wishes and are alert to the possibility of being checked on. Having seen the fitness levels and muscles of the club staff, Jay Jay was well aware he could have been dealt with rather severely had they been given any reason to suspect his motives. Their caution was, however, perhaps more related to the various drugs and stimulants they stocked, as this booming market had recently been the cause of a number of power struggles within the Kingdom. I myself had been involved in probing a little more deeply into the murder in Pattaya of a New Zealander who had just possibly been trying to undercut some rather more powerful suppliers. All in all, it was a very relieved Jay Jay who exited the club safe, sound and intact, vowing his days as an undercover agent in any gay bar, club or gay-oriented establishment were over once and for all.

A report was then compiled, all relevant footage put on a DVD and forwarded to the client, whom we assumed would, like any businessman deceived by a potential partner, be very quickly walking away from any future deals. So much for our assumptions. We received a reply shortly thereafter telling us that when he questioned lover-boy, the lad claimed he had only gone to the club as he wanted to surprise his generous sponsor on his return to Bangkok with a fitter and more attractive body.

Our client closed by asking if we could suggest a good lawyer to help him set up the proposed salon. We did think of asking him to update us with the location of the business so we could send an associate along for a facial, but I don't think Jay Jay would have seen the coy humour in that gesture.

WHERE THERE'S A WILL

"The truth is sometimes harder to discover than a lie is to uncover ... Therefore, if the truth is really so important that it enables that person seeking it to answer nagging questions and move on with their life, then surely it is priceless."

Thai Private Eye maxim

Let me start this chapter with a joke that seems quite fitting to the story that follows:

A Mafia Godfather finds out that his bookkeeper has cheated him out of ten million dollars. His bookkeeper is deaf, the reason he got the job in the first place. It was assumed that a deaf bookkeeper would not hear anything that he might later have to testify about in court. The Godfather goes to confront the bookkeeper about his missing $10 million, and brings along his lawyer, who also knows sign language. The Godfather tells the lawyer to ask him where the 10 million dollars is.

The lawyer, using sign language, duly asks the bookkeeper

what he did with the money. The bookkeeper signs back that he doesn't know what he's talking about. The lawyer relays this to the Godfather, who then pulls out a pistol, puts it the bookkeeper's temple and says, "Ask him again!"

The Lawyer signs to the bookkeeper that he will be killed if he doesn't come clean. The bookkeeper signs back, "Okay! You guys win! The money is in a brown briefcase, buried behind the shed in my backyard."

The Godfather asks the Lawyer what he said. The lawyer replies, "He says you don't have the balls to pull the trigger."

The story that follows is not at all funny though. What I am about to detail here is the final case in this book, and perhaps even the final one I'll ever be actively involved in. It is very current; in fact, it is still ongoing. It also happens to be somewhat "close-to-home" for me. Again, I can confirm that like all the others cases in this book, it is based totally on fact, but as you will understand in this case particularly, some names, locations and descriptions had to be altered due to the suspicions raised as well as the ongoing nature of investigations.

Over a decade ago, a simple Thai family lived in one of the cheaper areas of Bangkok. The husband was a chauffeur while his wife stayed home and cared for their three daughters. Their problems started one night when the husband came home rather late, rather drunk, and assumed, perhaps quite rightly, that his wife was having an affair with a neighbour.

The man had a handgun in his house, which he took with him as he went to confront the neighbour. In the ensuing fracas, the gun went off and the neighbour was badly injured, although not fatally. The police were called, and in due course, the chauffeur was sentenced to five years imprisonment.

Things then became even more difficult for the family, and so the oldest daughter, who was then 19 and earning a meagre salary in a clothing factory, was encouraged by her mother to find a far more financially rewarding job – in a local massage parlour.

Not too long thereafter, and presumably at her new place of work, the daughter met a somewhat older foreigner, who, as it happened, came from New Zealand. Although I never got to meet the man, I did get to know of him. This came as a result of one of those coincidences that seem to occur regularly in the Land of Smiles: When I married my Thai girlfriend some six or seven years after the above-mentioned massage parlour meeting, I learnt that my new wife was a relative of the family at the centre of this story. Hence my knowledge and understanding of the case. As well as my heightened interest.

The man involved was a quiet, unassuming fellow who had spent his lifetime in the army and, in fact, was not too far away from retirement. He was no front-line, gun-toting officer, however. In fact, he was much more of a backroom boy, having even completed a law degree whilst in the army. His army duties were actually more in the field of law and related areas of adjudication.

However, he had no immediate family.

This fine gentleman became very fond of the younger girl, learnt something of her story, and as happens so often, wanted to help her and get her into a better field of employment. He rented her a nice apartment, sent her to learn English, spent all his holidays with her, and also sent her a monthly retainer.

Approximately a year later, there was a major development: the girl became pregnant. Our army officer was happy at the prospect of his impending fatherhood, and so did all he could financially to help. He also confirmed that when he reached retirement age in another four or five years, he would settle permanently in Thailand. As the girl expressed a wish to be at home with her mother and younger sisters to help during her pregnancy, he found a better place of accommodation for them, and shortly thereafter, the former masseuse gave birth to a daughter.

The little girl was fine and healthy, and all seemed well. Unfortunately, however, this appears to be a family continually beset by disaster. Not too long after the birth, a wayward taxi driven by a drunk driver hit the baby girl's mother as she was walking along the road to her home, killing her.

Though obviously very upset, there was not really too much the army man could do. He had no family of his own to care for the little one, and so naturally enough, she was then placed in the care of her grandmother, who brought her up as her own. Of course, this upbringing was helped by a steady stream of funds, and visits, from her elderly Kiwi father.

In due course, when the girl was around seven years old, the father's time in the army was up, and he was discharged, leaving with substantial payments and pensions. With little better to do, he kept his word and relocated to Thailand. Rather than live on the outskirts of Bangkok in a Thai-only neighbourhood, he decided to base himself down the highway, in Pattaya. There are a large number of expats living in this resort town, and the shopping malls, supermarkets and even hospitals there are very Westernised. All of which made the retired officer's transition that much easier.

He soon found a nice home on the outskirts of Pattaya, expensive by local standards: 3 million Thai baht. But the home had all the modern conveniences, even a swimming pool. He was soon introduced by the estate agent to a local lawyer, who completed the details. Upon learning of the man's background, the lawyer became something of a local advisor to him. (The lawyer's willingness to help was no doubt spurred by the New Zealander's ability to buy such an expensive home. Now I'm not saying the law firm was the fabled Dewey, Screwem and Howe, but that does give you some idea as to how they are viewed in that part of the world!)

Our now happily retired officer had regular visits from his daughter and saw that she had the best of schooling, and that her family also had money for food and clothing. (Although in many instances, it is possible that some of the food and clothing money got diverted into alcoholic beverages and gambling.)

His new lawyer friend was happy to advise him on interests or activities to get involved in, and actually came up with a wonderful opportunity. This was the chance to join with the lawyer's brother-in-law, a Danish chap, who was in the process of setting up a small menagerie or zoo where local and visiting youngsters could both learn about and get up close to Thailand's native plants, animals and reptiles.

Having a young daughter of his own, this greatly appealed to the New Zealander, and he clearly felt that travelling around Thailand and collecting the many exotic animals and reptiles was going to be an interesting and rewarding experience. Plans were then drawn up, the land had already been purchased, and the infrastructure work begun. As the Dane's funds had waned, new investors were required, and in the retired army man, he had seemingly found a perfect and enthusiastic partner. In a further act of helpfulness, the Dane's Thai wife had introduced the Kiwi to an older auntie, apparently a qualified nurse, who was happy to accompany their new partner on his travels. This was advisable, as the New Zealander was finding the heat rather exhausting at times, and perhaps his health overall was starting to fail a little.

He arranged shortly thereafter for all his own funds and investments to be cashed up and transferred to Thailand, and he invested most of this into the new venture. He had a lifetime army pension that was now paid into his Thai account, and this more than covered his regular living expenses.

These are the facts that I've uncovered bit by bit as I have worked through the case over the past few months. There were, in addition, two further very important facts that came to light. During one of the daughter's regular weekend stays with her father and his new companion/ friend/ personal nurse, the trio had spent a day at the renowned Chatujack market and purchased a number of Thai water dragons, iguanas and even a snapping tortoise, which were temporarily being kept in the backyard of their home, awaiting permanent residence in the soon-to-be completed zoo.

Over that weekend, the daughter had developed a fever, so as a precaution, she had been taken to the local hospital. At his nurse/companion's request, and unbeknown to her father, a blood sample and associated DNA test were also requested at that time.

Sometime after the hospital invoice was presented and test results finalized (perhaps when the New Zealander was discussing the future or inheritances with her), the nurse produced the DNA result, no doubt brushing it off as a standard test run by Thai hospitals. The test confirmed what perhaps deep down he had always known: he was not the little girl's biological father.

Just how this affected him, I will never know. He certainly cared very much for the little girl, and no doubt saw much of the girl's mother in her. Perhaps, however, he harboured the feeling that the girl's grandmother and her aunties, whom he had provided for very admirably over the years, had known the truth all along and had to some extent hidden that knowledge and abused his trust.

The other fact to emerge from my research was even more tragic, especially as far as our benevolent Kiwi was concerned. A short time later, he was found dead in his own swimming pool by the nurse/companion, supposedly when she returned home from a shopping expedition. Even allowing for the fact that he was ailing, the death was most unexpected. Furthermore, it was a few days after the event that the man's young daughter and her family were first notified, and, as I found out later, no postmortem was ever undertaken, or in fact even considered. The best official version I can get is that he had been unwell, he was old, and it was believed he had a heart attack whilst swimming alone in his pool and subsequently drowned. Death by natural causes?

As I have found with deplorable regularity in similar instances, especially, it seems, cases that happen in Pattaya, there was a surprising lack of cash, gold or even bank funds left by the deceased. The rather swift funeral arrangements and subsequent cremation were carried out by the lawyer, who was assisted by the now late New Zealander's former business partner.

I ran some quick background checks on the Dane, who, it appeared, had a number of debts around town. However, it was noted that most of these debts had just recently been cleared. Certainly his night-time activities showed no signs of remorsefulness, or even of abating, but did indicate that he maintained a fairly expensive lifestyle.

Requests for information or statements regarding the business venture remain unanswered, and a mention that perhaps the young girl is the retired officer's only and rightful heir resulted in my being informed that he was not, in fact, her biological father. It was also mentioned that there was little money in the estate anyway. Just how this Danish businessman was privy to all this information ... well, you connect the dots yourself, but a close link between lawyer, business partner and the companion/nurse seems all too evident. It certainly looks like a conspiracy, smells like a conspiracy, so more than likely it is a conspiracy. But how can I prove it?

I called on what little authority I can muster in what I consider the quasi-cesspool that is Pattaya. Shortly after my contacts in authority made one or two enquiries into the death and subsequent events, lo and behold, a sudden payment from the lawyer was forwarded to the Thai family. No doubt, this was an attempt to placate what is a rather poor, and possibly very gullible, family. While obviously they were happy with the windfall, it has only served to further fuel my own suspicions.

The girl's grandmother, who is also her legal guardian, and her two aunties each received a payment of 100,000 Thai baht, far more than any of them would ever earn in a year, but seen in the light of the man's estate, not that much. What, however, was even more suspect is that those payments were made to the women's Thai nicknames. While the correct family names were on the payment cheques, instead of using their full and correct names (which the deceased man would have undoubtedly known), whoever wrote out the cheques used the women's nicknames.

This is something along the lines of leaving money to Posh, Sporty and Ginger Spice. Would an army man, a former lawyer himself, a stickler for correct procedure and doing things by the book, make out a will leaving things to Miss Chubby and Miss Crab when he undoubtedly knew their correct names as listed on their passports, or official Thai documents?

Also proving something of a mystery is the so-called nurse. She was around for the initial few days following the death, and briefly met the deceased man's little daughter and her family from visits in happier times. She was also aware that they came down to Pattaya immediately on being given news of the man's passing. Shortly after that, however, the nurse disappeared.

I can find no trace of her leaving the country, although it is still today a simple matter to cross the border into Laos, Cambodia or Malaysia covertly. Also, Thailand is a very easy country in which to live quietly in an upcountry village and have limited contact with the outside world. Enquiries confirm that she is not wanted by police for any questioning, and the death and subsequent events are not being treated as suspicious. It is, to all intents and purposes, a closed case. Well, a closed case to all except one meddling private eye!

The only solid information I have received is from the New Zealand side of this tangled web. There, any death must go to probate, and any estate over $10,000 must be passed through a high court. That information then becomes public, so I will shortly be able to trace what happened from this end. However, as to his house and investments in Thailand, things are looking increasingly murky.

The company that had been set up in Pattaya to construct and ultimately run the zoo had, as required under Thai Law, the minimum slate of seven directors, each with equal powers. Again, as is required by Thai law, four of the seven had to be Thai nationals. Was the deceased fully aware of this? I rather doubt it.

The Thai lawyer, his wife, the Dane's Thai wife, and an office worker who was also a relation are shown on the company documentation as the Thai participants. They were joined by our late army man, the Dane and a British man I am still trying to locate. I would guess the Briton and the now deceased New Zealander were the major financial contributors, and they probably believed they had at least a half share in the company and had no idea they could be out-voted at any time. It has further become obvious that almost all of the deceased man's rather ample funds I can track have found their way into the would-be zoological company's account.

A closer look at the company records, held at the registrar

in Rachada, shows it was, in fact, formed at the same time as my fellow Kiwi was buying his Pattaya mansion. Further investigation has shown that the proposed site is today somewhat overgrown scrubland, with no signs of development, and is, indeed, up for sale. Looking into the history of the land also proved interesting. It just happened to be previously owned by that Pattaya lawyer, who had, in turn, sold it to the zoo company the day after said company was formed.

Thus, the intrigues of investigations in Thailand and Southeast Asia continue, certainly often with more twists and turns than the more mundane cases my compatriots in the West usually face. As to the outcome of the above, well I shall attempt to keep you informed. I will add a note to the Thai Private Eye website should anything positive eventuate. For now, however, it poses a number of unsettling questions and reeks of fraud, corruption, and perhaps even murder. Unfortunately, many such cases in this region do just get filed away and closed, unanswered questions and all.

I now think back to my very beginnings as a private eye, to my days in that upcountry hotel where it all started, and the fact that no one was ever charged or sought in connection with Uncle's death. No I wonder if what is perhaps my last case is destined to end in a similar manner. Should that happen, I guess I will just have to take solace in the fact that amongst the numerous Thai traits and beliefs I have adopted over the years, *wen gum* – the

Buddhist belief that doing bad deeds will come back to haunt you later in life – may still prove true in this particular instance.

ACKNOWLEDGMENTS

I would like to especially thank the man who is now in charge at Thai Private Eye (and wishes to remain anonymous) for his help and friendship and for "casting an eye" over the more recent cases as I worked through them.

My thanks also go out to those at Monsoon, especially Phil, who has been a great help to me in this somewhat different field (for me anyway) of writing and publication, and also Richard Lord, who as my editor had the sometimes unenviable task of putting clarity and tighter organisation into my occasionally wayward ramblings.

Rob, the "wingman", and other friends on our special forum have all offered advice and support. So to them also, my sincere thanks. Locally, PK, a close and valued friend, always there for my family and me: your support greatly appreciated. And, of course, my wife Goong, who does her best and helped me now, as she has done for many years, with her insight on things Thai, as seen from her perspective. And most of all, my daughter Natalie, who motivates me these days, and who is a daily reminder of the bright and beautiful things that can come out of the Land of Smiles.

CONFESSIONS OF A BANGKOK PRIVATE EYE

True stories from the case files
of Warren Olson

Warren Olson & Stephen Leather

'Two-timing bargirls, suspicious spouses
and lesbian lovers – it was all in a day's work for Bangkok Private
Eye Warren Olson.'

For more than a decade Olson walked the mean streets of the
Big Mango. Fluent in Thai and Khamen, he was able to go where
other Private Eyes feared to tread.

His clients included Westerners who had lost their hearts
– and life savings – to money-hungry bargirls. Nobody knows
more than Warren Olson abou tthe tricks that bargirls can use to
separate Western men from their hard-earned money. But he had
more than his fair share of Thai clients, too, including a sweet old
lady who was ripped off by a Christian conman and a Thai girl
blackmailed by a former lover.

The stories are based on Olson's case files, fictionalised (to
protect the innocent, and the guilty) by bestselling author Stephen
Leather.

ISBN: 978-981-05-4832-2

(www.monsoonbooks.com.sg/bookpage_0548322.html)